For You

Andreas Seidl

Handover of Power

European Version

Volume 12: Finance

Imprint

Bibliographic information of the German National Library:
The German National Library lists this publication in the
German National Bibliography; detailed bibliographic data
are available on the Internet at http://dnb.dnb.de.

© 2022 Dipl. Pol. Theodor Andreas Seidl

Cover: Christiane Ebrecht
Translation: DeepL, Cologne
Production and publishing: BoD – Books on Demand,
Norderstedt

ISBN: 978-3-7568-0261-6

Acknowledgements

My thanks go to my family and friends who have made me who I am today. Special thanks to all those who supported me in writing this book. I would like to thank all my classmates, teachers, fellow students, lecturers, demonstrators, activists, colleagues, companies and countries with whom I have had the privilege of sharing the experiences from which all the ideas in this book have emerged. I would like to thank the staff of Books on Demand for their kind helpfulness. I thank the citizens of Seligenstadt for the harmony and solidarity in which I was able to write.

Foreword

This policy concept contains a variety of proposals for possible political reforms. It can be peacefully and democratically adapted to any current political system of any state in the world, but also to political systems in families, clubs, associations or companies. Wherever humans make or submit to rules that manage living together, the following proposals can be helpful. Readers who find the proposals so helpful that they would like to implement them together with like-minded people can contact the author. The contact form on the last page can be used for this purpose.

Faults and defects
I ask for your understanding that this volume was not professionally proofread. I could only afford professional proofreading for the summary. Spelling errors and unfortunate phrasing may therefore occur. As soon as this volume has sold enough to pay for a professional proofreading, it will be done. After that, a new edition will be published.

English version
Please understand that this volume has been translated automatically. I could only afford a professional translation for the summary. Poor wording and spelling errors may therefore occur. In case of doubt, the German version shall prevail. As soon as this volume has sold enough to pay for a professional translation, it will be done. After that, a new edition will be

published. It was more important to me that no one in the world should have an information advantage than individual translation errors in the complete work.

References
If something has been quoted directly, it is set in italics. If the headings contain footnotes, the sources for direct and indirect quotations apply in the chapter for which the heading stands. Otherwise, quotations or source references are directly at the word or at the end of the sentence or paragraph. This book contains parts of text based on the Federal Constitution of the Swiss Confederation of 18 April 1999 (as of 12 February 2017), abbreviated to BV[1] and the Constitution of the Canton of Bern of 6 June 1993 (as of 11 March 2015), abbreviated to KV[2] .

If the constitutional paragraph, or individual paragraphs thereof, are based in whole or in part on extracts from the BV or KV, this is indicated in a footnote. The references to the corresponding footnotes for constitutional paragraphs are usually found after the heading of the affected chapter and sometimes in the body of the text. Articles used in the Swiss constitutions are listed in the footnote with a number after the title of the constitutional paragraph. Example: §123 Sample title: BV Art.123, KV Art.123.

All internet sources are fully cited in the footnotes. They were last accessed on 30.09.2021. All literature sources are also listed in full in the footnotes.

All references to tasks undertaken by other ministries and described in more detail there are given in footnotes. Example: Model Ministry - 1.2.3 Model Chapter.

All footnotes are to be viewed in comparison to the respective source, so-called indirect quotations. Direct quotations are set in italics, but hardly ever occur. The source reference is intended to enable further investigation and to take copyright

---

[1] This is not an official publication. Only the publication by the Swiss Federal Chancellery is authoritative. https://www.fedlex.admin.ch/eli/cc/1999/404/de On 14.12.2021

[2] This is not an official publication. The Bernese Official Collection of Laws is authoritative. https://www.belex.sites.be.ch/frontend/versions/2420?locale=de#ART71 On 16.12.2021

into account.

All keywords used, based on the names of the responsible units, departments and ministries of Germany, are listed at the end of this volume in the chapter on the conversion of ministries.

Table of contents

1 Goals of the Ministry of Finance

All the objectives of the Ministry of Finance are to give the people power over the state's financial resources. The people are given the power to determine revenues through laws and expenditure through the budget vote.

One of the objectives of the Ministry of Finance is to administer the revenues and expenditures of the state in a way that is at least balanced and as profitable as possible. With the help of taxes, the People's Bank, Central Bank, Note-issuing Banks and the Audit Court, the budget is monitored and used for the benefit of the people. To make the responsibility for the people clear, the Finance Minister and the heads of the People's Bank, Central Bank, Note-issuing Banks and the Audit Court are directly elected. Full employment, stable prices, long-term growth in the standard of living, the constant support of the people with means of payment, low taxes and fees, and protection against economic crises are goals pursued by the Ministry of Finance. The Ministry of Finance is increasingly saying goodbye to the goal of full employment, in the same measure of advancing automation. It supports a sufficient supply of means of payment through the Unconditional Basic Income.

In order to keep the work comprehensible to the people, the Ministry of Finance organises the budget management in an entrepreneurial and direct-democratic way. The cost-covering prices with a profit mark-up for state services are entrepreneurial, the annual budget vote is direct-democratic.

2 Departments

The departments are divided into sub-departments and enumerations are usually considered as their individual units. Many tasks of some departments are completely taken over by other ministries as a service.

2.1 Central Department

Part of the Central Department is the Reception Office with the Courier and Mail Room, which directs all concerns, broadcasts and visitors to the appropriate place in the ministry.

2.1.1 Staff

The Human Resources Department is responsible for staff development and planning. For this purpose, it takes care of the recruitment of junior staff, intern and trainee programmes as well as the selection procedures for employees and special selection procedures for applicants with disabilities. For politicians and employees, the department prepares a job plan. In all its tasks, it works in voting with the personnel board.[1]
All other personnel matters are transferred to the respective ministries. The Ministry of Education is responsible for the training and further education of employees for the state service.[2] The Ministry of Labour takes over the service law.[3] This includes the labour and collective bargaining law for employees in the state service, remuneration, personnel administration of all careers and employees, flexitime, holiday and sickness records, working time with or without flexitime in part-time or full-time at the place of work or in home work. The Ministry of Infrastructure provides housing assistance for all state employees.[4]
The Ministry of Education provides childcare for all employees in the state service.[5]
The Ministry of Health is responsible for the occupational health service.[6] It ensures occupational health management, deals with the treatment, education and prevention of occupational accidents, controls and provides occupational

---

1 Ministry of State Organisation - 2.1.1.1 Personnel board
2 Ministry of Education - 2.1.1.1 Education and training for the state service
3 Ministry of Labour - 4 State enterprises, 13 Labour Directory
4 Ministry of Infrastructure - 2.1.1.1 Housing assistance for state service employees
5 Ministry of Education - 2.1.1.2 Childcare for state service employees
6 Ministry of Health - 2.1.1.1 Occupational Health Service

health and safety through the health auditors[7] of the Company Auditing Agency[8] .

2.1.1.1 Staff remuneration

In the Pay Office, salary, expenses, travel costs and relocation costs for all ministries are settled directly with the employees through their account at the People's Bank. For this purpose, the Ministry of Finance provides all state employees with a request for payment application via their current account. The employees have to fill out the application and are automatically transferred the specified amount. A copy of the application is sent to the affected ministry and to the Ministry of Finance's payroll office, which sorts the application and the remittance slip into the ministry's expenses to be audited by the audit services.

2.1.2 Organisation

The ministries of media, security, justice, finance, labour, state organisation provide audit services for quality management in the ministry, evaluation of work performance, revenues and expenditures, as well as corruption prevention, sabotage protection and, if necessary, disciplinary matters.[9]
The Ministry of Labour regulates procurement law and ensures corruption-free state orders and procurement.[10] The Ministry of Education is in charge of the language service for translating conversations or texts.[11]
The Ministry of Digital Affairs supports the supply of Information Technology.[12] In voting with the Procurement Office of the Ministry of Labour, it takes care of the procurement, provision, maintenance and service of technical

---

7 Ministry of Labour - 20.7.2 Health auditor
8 Ministry of Labor - 20 Company Auditing Agency
9 Ministries of Media, Security, Justice, Finance, State Organisation - 2.1.2.1 Audit services
10 Ministry of Labour - 6 Procurement Office
11 Ministry of Education - 2.1.3 Language Service
12 Ministry of Digital Affairs - 2.1.2.1.1 Supply of Information Technology

devices and software. Much of this is produced in-house to ensure data protection in information and communication technology. Information technology and digitalisation officers audit and advise the ministries. Digital appointment calendar and documentation services are provided as well as a digital policy archive including a library.

2.1.2.1 Audit services

The Ministry of Finance uses its tax auditors to check whether funds have been improperly used, embezzled or evaded. They are deployed in the annual audit of the Company Auditing Agency[13] and in the monitoring team of the Surveillance Television. The Audit Court is another independent audit service. The audits examine the account movements of citizens, activities of companies and ministries. These audits are used for quality management and protection against sabotage, as well as for evaluating the circulation of money and preventing corruption. If violations are found, this results in disciplinary matters, the course of which and compliance with them are also examined.

2.1.2.2 Budget management

The budget procedure and budget law are regulated in the chapters on state revenues, tax policy, budget consolidation and state expenditure. The personnel budget, departmental budgets, costs and treasury are settled via the state account at the People's Bank. All cost centres flow into the budget planning for the coming budget vote as forecasts for revenues and expenditures in the coming year. The Tax Office is responsible for the budget management of all ministries.

---

13 Ministry of Labor - 20 Company Auditing Agency

2.2 Management Department

The Management Department is the minister's department. With his office team, he provides policy planning and analysis for his ministry and coordinates the relationship between the nation and the municipality through exchanges with his deputies in the municipalities. He initiates cooperation with other ministries or citizens in committees and is supported by the Ministry of State Organisation.

The Ministry of Media Affairs, through its media service, provides press and public relations for the ministry, moderates civil dialogue, trains or provides a spokesperson for the minister, writes speeches and texts on request, and ensures the implementation of conferences and events.[14]

The Ministry of Digital Affairs is responsible for digital management and thus provides departmental management. It automatically produces business statistics, staff surveys and the current state of research through statistics. It automatically forwards proposals to the affected or empowered state employees. In document management, it ensures digitalisation and that ministries share forms with each other.[15]

2.3 European Department

The Ministry of Foreign Affairs ensures the constant transmission of the latest information on current European policy affecting the ministry concerned, applicable European Union law and all European Union funding programmes starting or in progress.[16]

The European Department, in cooperation with the Ministry of Foreign Affairs, ensures compliance with and formulation of the European rules on the budget of the Member States and the entire European Union, as well as joint harmonisation of taxes and prosecution of tax fraud. It coordinates cooperation between the Ministry of Free Market Economy, the European Central Bank and the Note-issuing Bank of the Free Market Economy.

14 Ministry of Media Affairs - 2.2.1.1 Media Service
15 Ministry of Digital Affairs - 2.1.2.1 Digital Service
16 Ministry of Foreign Affairs - 2.4 European Department

The European Department decides for the areas of budget[17] , taxation[18] , economy and currency[19] , whether current European Union law is adopted, adapted or rejected.[20]

2.4 Budget Department

The Budget Department operates the Tax Office. In cooperation with the People's Bank, Company Auditing Agency and the Ministries of Labour and Economic Affairs, it coordinates the levying and moving in of business taxes, value added taxes, taxes on assets and tariffs. For tariffs, the department additionally cooperates with the Ministry of Security. It coordinates the payment of Unconditional Basic Income and the reduction of taxes.

It oversees the Unconditional Basic Income, Automation and Business Cycle Compensation funds. It coordinates fiscal consolidation procedures with the municipalities and ministries. It ensures the aggregation of all necessary data from the ministries to calculate their revenues from taxes, fees, assets, profits and debts on a monthly basis.

It coordinates the timely and complete submission of the ministries' financial plans and hands over the draft budget to the cabinet. In cooperation with all ministries, it organises the budget committee, the election campaign and the budget vote for the distribution of state expenditure. It ensures the digital requirements for measuring and distributing state expenditure in cooperation with the ministries of digital and media.

It monitors the independence of the Audit Court and is obliged to provide it with all data that it can also inspect or generate.

17https://eur-lex.europa.eu/summary/chapter/budget.html?root_default=SUM_1_CODED=06

18https://eur-lex.europa.eu/summary/chapter/taxation.html?root_default=SUM_1_CODED=21

19https://eur-lex.europa.eu/summary/chapter/economic_and_monetary_affairs.html?root_default=SUM_1_CODED=14

20Ministry of Foreign Affairs - 6.4 Conversion of political contents to the policy of dynamic media democracy

2.5 Finance Department

The Finance Department ensures the operation of the Central Bank, Note-issuing Banks and the People's Bank. In cooperation with the Ministries of Labour and Economic Affairs, it drafts legislation for the Central Bank, Note-issuing Banks and the People's Bank. The Finance Department, in cooperation with the Company Auditing Agency, is responsible for supervising the financial institutions to ensure that they comply with the applicable laws and calculate the economic ratios correctly. Otherwise, it safeguards the independence of the Central Bank and Note-issuing Banks from non-state or foreigner interests and the autonomy of their directly elected heads. It reports doubts to the Minister of Finance, who can intervene in the work of the monetary institutions with the majority approval of his deputies or the people.

The People's Bank has a special role because it is not independent, but is used by the citizens and ministries in their interest. The Finance Department coordinates the People's Bank's relations with the other ministries and the citizens. It oversees the operation of the People's Stock Exchange and the Ideas Stock Exchange, as well as the management of funds for the people, real estate and foreign investors, and whether the work of the Investment Department complies with the law.

3 Tasks of the Ministry of Finance

The ministry is responsible for financial, economic and tax policy. In doing so, it coordinates its policies with the ministries of labour and economy. Especially the structural issues of tax policy are clarified with the ministries of economy in order to ensure a consistent structure through the existence of all four economic forms. Based on the data collected, the Ministry of Finance conducts research in order to be able to estimate taxes, make analyses of the economy, monitor the growth of the money supply, the Living Standard Index and state revenues, and intervene if necessary.

The task of the Ministry of Finance is to ensure the sustainability of financial, economic and tax policies among citizens, companies and ministries. Sustainability is considered to be at risk if one or more economic forms suffer an economic downturn, cases of illness accumulate, the intranet cannot guarantee its legally secure networking, the infrastructure is dilapidated, occupational safety is at risk or innovations are delayed. It is the task of the Ministry of Finance, together with the Ministries of Economy, Health, Digital Affairs, Infrastructure, Labour and Innovation, to clarify where the cause lies and whether too little or too much money plays a role in the cause. If money plays a significant role, the Ministry of Finance is responsible for remedying the situation. If citizens file a complaint before an administrative court, the Constitutional Court or the European Court of Human Rights, which is related to the tasks of the Ministry of Finance, the Minister of Finance is considered the defendant. The national budget is administered by the Ministry of Finance. This includes collecting the revenues from taxes, profits and debts or savings, checking them and disbursing the revenues to the ministries. The disbursement is made according to the distribution decided in the annual budget vote.

3.1 Theory of the state as a company

Analogous to the theory of the state as an entrepreneur of the national economy[21] , the Ministry of Finance occupies a key position to fulfil the idea of a democratically run company. The basic state organisation resembles the organisational structure of a company, or rather a corporation with a parent company that administers the revenues and many subsidiaries that generate the revenues and thereby also consume part of the revenues as costs. The Ministry of Finance takes on the role of the parent company and ensures that the state budget can post an annual profit, but is at least balanced.

This form of enterprise must be thought of as if there were subsidiaries that work for the market, i.e. for the people, and other subsidiaries that are service providers for the parent company, for example the Ministry of Digital Affairs when Information Technology is affected.

---

21 Ministry of State Organisation - 5.3 Theory of the state as an economic entrepreneur

The Ministry of Finance's responsibilities are comparable to accounting or operational controlling, because the Ministry of Finance is responsible for liquidity and budget management. The other part of operational controlling, namely the provision of information, is taken over by the Ministry of Finance with its intranet site and the People's Bank's online account access together with the Ministry of Digital Affairs and the Ministry of Media Affairs. Comparable to strategic controlling, the Ministry of Innovation is responsible for new markets and the Company Auditing Agency is responsible for risk assessment, market assessment and tax auditing.

3.1.1 Citizens as consumers, owners and workers

Citizens play three roles in the state as a company. The largest group are the citizens who are consumers of the services that the state provides. The second largest group is the citizens as voters, who sit on the board of directors and the board of directors, so to speak, in order to have numbers, persons, products, services or laws that are part of state services presented to them by politicians and managers alike. The third largest group is the citizens as state employees, who are politicians or state employees.

Every citizen can determine through his or her gainful employment in an economic form whether and which state services are Tax-funded for him or her or are only available as a more expensive individual service.

3.1.2 Economic cycle

The circuit is as follows. Through its revenues, the state, with the help of its ministries, provides services and conditions that the citizens use to live and the companies use to work. This generates revenues, firstly by the ministries setting prices and making profits for their individual services, secondly by People's Innovation Company[22] making monopoly profits on the world market, and thirdly by taxes on citizens and

22 Ministry of Innovation - 10 People's Innovation Company

companies.

Each ministry and all its offices and authorities are in a position to generate profits and to be able to plan a part of these profits themselves. Profit-sharing for employees rewards performance and independent entrepreneurial action within the state service.

It becomes clear that, on the one hand, this state as a company markets its services directly, because state employees provide services that they offer for purchase or as a subscription. On the other hand, it creates conditions for citizens to live and work together. This increases the number of citizens, which increases value added taxes. In companies, citizens participate in the creation of value, which increases business taxes. Self-employment under the law is most similar to the well-known franchise company. The parent company gives certain requirements and otherwise allows the franchisees to decide many things independently, but to have to pay a share of the turnover or profits to the parent company.

3.1.3 Advantages

The conditions for economic governance are more favourable if the state manages its budget in an entrepreneurial manner. The prerequisite for entrepreneurial governance is, firstly, that companies have established reliable structures in order to cover costs with revenues and to be able to generate profits in the long term. Secondly, that companies and their leadership are better known to the citizen than bureaucratic leadership. Thirdly, that companies can be neatly separated but still work together in an alliance, making it possible to connect the national, municipal and private levels more productively. Fourth, that companies have developed techniques to compete internationally that will be useful in the future international competition between states. Fifth, that companies are primarily concerned with covering costs and only secondarily with prestige, which distinguishes the entrepreneur from the politician.

3.1.4 Goals

The goal of the state as a company is a low suicide rate, a high birth rate, a high age, an educated and rich population, so that the continuity of the company is secured and the standard of living of humanity increases in the long term through technical progress. Debt and bad investments, on the other hand, bring the state as a company closer to bankruptcy or into dependency on foreign powers. Both endanger the existence of the state and can be prevented by controlling and accounting. Money conceals the greatest potential for a hostile takeover by other states or persons. Keeping this danger away from the people must be a condition of every action of the Ministry of Finance.

The goal is to achieve profits with the national economy that improve the lives of the people, because taxes are reduced and the proportion of weekly working hours steadily decreases until an Unconditional Basic Income can cover the cost of living and the pure desire to invent and discover steadily increases the standard of living of humanity and thus makes long-term sustainable growth in peace possible.

4 Tax Office

The Tax Office is located in the capital city of the Ministry of Finance, manages the revenues and expenditures of the ministries as well as the moving in of taxes. This includes firstly the control of proper moving in cooperation with the tax auditors of the Company Auditing Agency and the Tax Investigation Department. Secondly, the Tax Office, in cooperation with the People's Bank Investment Department, invests the taxes in the safest possible yet high-yielding financial products on the People's or Ideas Stock Exchange, while saving them for the coming financial year. Third, the Tax Office is responsible for publishing the state revenues before the budget vote so that ministries can prepare their financial plans.

5 Tax policy[23]

Tax policy is designed to provide revenues, to tax companies of different economic forms differently and to manage consumption, investment, production and foreign trade. The tax system consists only of value added taxes, business taxes and tariffs, if necessary also taxes on assets.

Any tax applies to the whole community and must not favour individuals. For this reason, taxes are calculated as a percentage and are not levied equally on everyone as fixed amounts. By levying taxes as a percentage, the economic productive capacity of each individual is taken into account. In principle, taxes are only permissible if they are also able to manage a key figure of the national accounts. The decisive indicators are consumption, income, production, investment and foreign trade. If new taxes are to be introduced, they must be economically justified, must not tax anything twice and must be voted on by the people. To exclude double taxation, the ministries of labour, economy and foreigners must also agree before a new tax is introduced.

Automated tax management is done digitally through the tax accounts at People's Bank and the Tax Directory[24] . Tax auditing is carried out by the Company Auditing Agency during its regular audits of ministries and companies. In addition to the economic data, audits are also carried out to check whether accounting regulations and criminal tax law are being complied with.

5.1 Value added tax[25]

Value added tax is a consumer tax. Value added taxes are due on every commercial transaction between consumers or companies and consumers. For monetary payments, 20% of the amount payable is paid by the consumer. In the case of private consideration, the trade must be made through the People's Computer so that the value of the consideration is calculated and 20% of it is debited from the tax account.

23§148,1,2,3,6 Principles of taxation: BV Art.127, KV Art.104
24Ministry of Digital - 12 Directories
25§151 Value added tax: BV Art.130

Value added taxes are there to tax the final consumption of goods and services. This allows consumption to be managed by stimulating demand through a suggestion or curbing it through an increase. All value added tax revenues are booked to the Ministry of Finance account and allocated or saved in the subsequent budget vote.

Final consumers can be private individuals or companies at the end of the production and supply chain. All chargeable products that reach the consumer include value added tax. These include, for example, energy sources, fuel, electricity, food and beverages, insurance services, notarised deeds, telecommunications services such as internet, telephone and television, means of transport and transport services. State agencies do not pay value added tax on their chargeable services to each other.

To combat tax fraud, all VAT transactions of all tax accounts are automatically connected to each other in order to virtually recreate the value chain. If irregularities occur, the tax auditors are automatically alerted and start investigating.

5.1.1 Payment methods

If the payments are made digitally, the consumer's current account is debited, the payment flows through the company's tax account where 20% of the amount is paid to the Ministry of Finance and then to the company account.

Insofar as payments are made in cash, the VAT rate is already deducted when cash is withdrawn. The Note-issuing Banks and People's Bank ensure that every cash withdrawal from the account from ATMs, bank counters or supermarket checkouts is taxed at the VAT rate.

5.1.2 Scope

Value added tax is the same in all economic forms. The only exception is the Barter Economy, where mostly quid pro quos are the rule. Therefore, a lump sum of working hours is due that the consumer has to perform in the state service. This reduces state expenditure by the amount that would have been incurred if value added tax had been applied.

In foreign trade, value added tax is paid by domestic citizens on imported goods and services. Tariffs equal to the value added tax is levied on the export of goods and services.

5.2 Business tax[26]

Business taxes are taxes on income. They are there to tax the income from entrepreneurial activity of natural and legal persons. Either the turnover in the form of sales revenue or the profit in the form of sales revenue less costs is taxed. The records that the companies have to keep in their accounts are defined by the Ministry of Finance in the Balance Sheet Tax Law.

Business taxes vary depending on the economic form and are set by the respective Ministry of Economy. In the Social Market Economy and Planned Economy, profits are taxed, in the Free Market Economy and Barter Economy, turnover is taxed. Whether more or less business taxes are paid is directly related to how much freedom or security the state offers a company. In this respect, the companies also decide on the level of their business taxes through the election of their economic form.

If private individuals want to sell goods or offer services for which they receive money or consideration, they must register a company for this purpose, no matter how short the company exists. Sellers of goods and suppliers of services are liable for business tax. Those who accept cash in return must deposit it in their company account. Anyone who produces goods or provides services for themselves, their friends or family without receiving anything in return does not pay business tax.

26§150,2,5 Business taxes

5.2.1 Entrepreneurial activity

Entrepreneurial activity includes all possibilities to create added value from one's own actions. As soon as one takes the initiative and uses one's assets, consisting of money and things, to provide a paid service for persons or companies, one becomes an entrepreneur.

For example, dividends or interest income can be generated from securities, rent can be collected from real estate, a profit margin can be generated from a purchase and sale, or products can be sold profitably through a production or service including employees. Any increase in money is considered an entrepreneurial activity. An employment relationship is not an entrepreneurial activity. The costs of equipment, materials, human and machine labour are not taxed individually, but by the company as a whole. The machine tax of the Planned Economy is exempt from this.[27]

5.2.2 Business forms

Natural persons are persons who undertake a business in order to earn money. These are, for example, freelancers, small entrepreneurs or an entrepreneurial community. Legal persons are companies that provide services with an economic added value on the instructions of their owners and managing directors. These are, for example, corporations, cooperatives, clubs, institutions or foundations. Whether natural or legal persons earn money, they must open a company in the economic form of their election by creating a profile in the Labour Directory. This is followed by the automatic opening of a company account with People's Bank. On this account, one has at least the tax account, but can also open all other accounts of the People's Bank as sub-accounts and carry out all banking transactions of the company there.

---

27 Ministry of Planned Economy - 10.5.5 Machine tax

5.2.3 Cash

The companies must accept cash from customers and can make their purchases in cash. A cash fund must be created for this purpose. With the purpose "cash register", owners or managing directors can withdraw cash from the company account and must deposit it in their cash register. This cash can be used to hold change for customers on the one hand and to make purchases for the company on the other. For both uses, increased record keeping is required for the companies. For purchases, the time, date, place, quantity, price and name of the seller or selling company must be recorded in a cash register. Customers must have this data printed out as a receipt or transmitted digitally upon request. However, entrepreneurs may not use one and the same cash register to cash out customers and purchase goods or services for the company. A separate cash register must be acquired for each of the two transactions so that value added tax and business tax can be accounted for separately.

The cash registers are available through the Intranet Café and are produced by the Ministry of Digital Affairs.[28] They are connected to the Intranet and automatically transmit the data to the Ministry of Finance and to the company's profile in the Labour Directory.

Taking cash from the company's cash box for private consumption is prohibited. If cash is found to have been taken by the Company Auditing Agency, a court hearing will be held and, if convicted, an imprisonment in the amount of the money taken from the company's cash box will be imposed.[29]

5.2.4 Shares

Shares are treated by the tax law as a product that a company produces and sells. The nature of the product makes it possible for the owner to earn money with it through the dividend, which automatically makes him an entrepreneur and the dividend taxable. When a joint-stock company sells shares

28 Ministry of Digital Affairs - 13.6.9.2 Cash register
29 Ministry of Justice - 7.5.2 Assessment of the duration of detention

and when shareholders sell their shares, business tax is also due. In the case of a sales tax, the selling price is taxed; in the case of a profit tax, the difference between the selling price and the buying price is taxed.

The dividend counts directly as profits or turnover. As soon as the joint-stock company transfers the dividend, business taxes are deducted before the account is credited to the shareholder's account.

5.2.5 Sales tax

Free Market Economy and Barter Economy business tax is due on turnover and is payable immediately. For business accounts, all cash receipts are taxed. All cash receipts are taxed at the business tax rate set by the respective Ministry of Economy. Turnover is calculated by multiplying the price by the quantity sold. During the Company Auditing Agency audit, the quantities sold and the prices are recorded and reconciled with the tax account data. Tax is incurred even if there are losses. Losses cannot reduce the tax liability. If discrepancies become apparent, the Tax Investigation Department initiates investigations.

5.2.5.1 Example cash in circulation

For example, an entrepreneur in the Free Market Economy takes in 10 euros in cash. He pays the money into his company account and thus automatically pays business tax. There are now 8 euros in the company account, which he transfers to his private account. When he withdraws the 8 euros, he receives 6.40 euros at the ATM. When the money is paid into the company account, 20% Free Market Economy business tax has been deducted. When the money is paid out, 20% value added tax has been incurred.

5.2.6 Profit tax

With profit tax, all cash inflows and outflows of the company account are processed through the tax account. At the end of a month, it is calculated whether there were surpluses, which are taxed with profit tax. If there were losses or zero profits, no profit tax is due. If owners of a company are also employees, they do not receive wages, but profit sharing, which is paid out after tax deduction.

5.2.6.1 Example securities trading

For example, a shareholder sells a share from the Social Market Economy or Planned Economy. After deducting the costs for the stock exchange traders, the profits are calculated. It results from the sales price minus the purchase price of the share. From the profits, the shareholder pays the profit tax of the Social Market Economy or Planned Economy. For example, a shareholder has bought his share for 100 euros and sells it for 110 euros. If the joint-stock company comes from the Social Market Economy, 30% business tax is deducted. The former shareholder receives 7 euros in his savings account. If he withdraws the 7 euros, he pays 20% value added tax and receives 5.60 euros. The calculation would be the same if the dividend were 10 euros.

5.2.7 Business taxes in the economic forms[30]

The four ministries of economy, in voting with the Ministry of Finance, determine their respective corporate tax rates and whether sales taxes or profit taxes should be levied to adequately manage their economic form.

Tax revenues flow into the state budget. The people decide how much tax revenue may be used exclusively by the ministries of economy for their economic form.

Business taxes vary in the four economic forms and thus correspond to the different levels of state services provided to

---

30§148,4,5 Principles of taxation: KV Art.104, §150,1,3,4 Business taxes companies. In the Barter Economy, they are payable as sales tax on goods and services. Here, the state hardly builds any infrastructure and provides little support. Therefore, business taxes are lowest in the Barter Economy. In Planned Economy, they are levied as profit tax on exports. Exports are all sales to guests, tourists and exports to other economic forms. The state builds all the infrastructure, provides all the services that are in demand and thus ensures full employment. Therefore, business taxes are highest in Planned Economy. In the Social Market Economy, they are deducted monthly from the corporate tax account as profit tax, but not when losses are made. The state builds the necessary infrastructure and provides insurance. Business taxes are lower than in the Planned Economy and higher than in the Free Market Economy. In the Free Market Economy, they are immediately deducted as sales tax from all payments into the company account. The state only builds the infrastructure that is commissioned at a cost, charges fees for all services and ensures competitiveness. Business taxes in the Free Market Economy are lower than in the Social Market Economy and higher than in the Barter Economy.

5.2.7.1 Double taxation[31]

No company may be registered in several economic forms at the same time in order to avoid double taxation. Persons may operate several companies in different economic forms and pay the business taxes of the affected economic form for the respective company.

Foreign companies whose foreign country is in an international union with the domestic country and which operate in the domestic country may not be charged business tax in more than one member state. Business taxes are levied on the basis of the turnover or profits made inland. To avoid double taxation with a third country, taxation agreements must be negotiated with that foreign country. The Ministries of Finance, Labour, Economic Affairs and Foreign Affairs of all affected countries must be involved in the negotiations. As long as there are no

31 §148.6 Principles of taxation: BV Art.127, §153.3 Exclusion of double taxation: BV Art.134

agreements, double taxation is possible.

5.2.7.2 Tax harmonisation[32]

The tax liability is guaranteed without any gaps by transferring the tax liability to the affected Ministry of Economy as of the effective date of the change to another economic form. The effective date of the conversion may only be at the end of the month, so that the old economic form is responsible in the expiring month and the new economic form in the newly beginning month.

The ministries for economic affairs regulate in the procedural law when which changes are permissible for companies and how they must be carried out. In it, they can regulate the purchase and sale of financial products, goods and services as well as the entry and exit of companies and issue fees. The fees cover the costs that may arise in the affected economic form as a result of a switch.[33]

Conversion fraud is punishable under criminal tax law and is decided on a case-by-case basis.[34] Tax avoidance strategies are primarily precluded by suitable laws. If these means are not sufficient, a switching tax can be introduced.

5.2.7.3 Switching tax

In order to ensure fiscally fair economic conditions, a switching tax can be introduced. It should bring about harmonisation between the economic forms and ensure that no economic form lives at the expense of another or that persons enrich themselves from it. Nevertheless, anyone who discovers an enterprise policy that serves to generate profits from switching between economic forms, that plays the economic forms off against each other, so to speak, should report the situation to the Ministry of Finance.

The report is reviewed by the Company Auditing Agency and analysed together with the ministries of labour and economy.

32 §149 Tax harmonisation: BV Art.129
33 Ministries of Economy - Switching between economic forms
34 Ministry of Justice - 8.5.1 Taxes

In a subsequent committee, the results are presented and negotiated on which goods, services, assets or companies the switching tax should be levied and at what rate. If possible, a time limit on the switching tax should be made possible until laws make it unnecessary.

5.3 Tariffs[35]

Tariffs are a foreign trade tax. The ministries involved in the management of foreign trade through tariffs are Finance, Labour, Health, Foreigners, Security and Economy. The Ministry of Security is responsible for customs clearance at the country's external borders. Persons entering and leaving the country, as well as importing and exporting companies, must pay duty on their goods, services and capital at Customs before crossing the border.[36]

The Ministry of Foreign Affairs, in voting with the affected peoples, can make agreements on tariffs between the inland and other countries. It monitors with the staff of its embassies whether environmental and human rights are respected in the supply chains that apply inland, rather than abroad where part of the supply chain is located. The audit is carried out when goods are imported into the inland or produced abroad by domestic citizens. Embassies are also responsible for reporting whether domestic exports or foreign imports are impeding the development of the affected industry in the Country-of-destination. If this is the case, the tariffs will be increased.

The Ministry of Health sets standards for occupational safety and environmental protection in supply chains and products. It sets costs for goods that are harmful to humans and the environment and can only be rendered harmless through costly procedures. The cost of decontamination is added to the price of imported goods and increases Customs tariffs.

The Ministry of Labour ensures that full employment in the country is not jeopardised by foreign trade. It monitors sectors with increased unemployment and business failures and can impose tariffs on affected goods and services or restrict the

---

35§152 Tariffs: BV Art.133
36Ministry of Security - 8.2 Border Protection

immigration of guest workers or order the departure of guest workers.

The Ministry of Finance manages foreign trade via the tariffs in the sense of national accounts. It is responsible for a balanced or slightly positive foreign trade balance between imports and exports. It levies tariffs in the amount of the value added tax. The ministries of economy can also set their own requirements as to which goods and services are subject to tariffs and how high they should be. This enables the ministries of economy to manage foreign trade with other economic forms and foreigners.

5.3.1 Tariffs with emerging and developing countries[37]

Customs duties are due on the import and export of goods and capital, the amount of which corresponds to domestic taxes. The amount of the additional tariffs depends on the difference in the standard of living in the country to which the goods are exported or from which they are imported. This is to avoid exploiting other countries or foreign workers because their standard of living is lower. The exchange rate of the currency is used as a reference. These tariffs are levied in addition and decrease at the same rate as poverty in emerging and developing countries decreases. If individual sectors of the economy are hindered or even prevented from exporting by domestic citizens, these exports are subject to tariffs. The embassy in the developing country calculates the necessary amount of tariffs until an industry can be established in the developing country and informs Customs. Customs duties incurred in trade with developing countries flow into development aid.[38]

---

37 §152.3 Tariffs
38 Ministry of Foreign Affairs - 8.7 Financing of development aid

5.4 Tax on assets

Taxes on assets are only used to reduce the debt of the following generation. If a generation has accumulated national debt that has not been paid off after 10 years, inheritances, gifts and annually on land are taxed. The tax rate depends on the amount of debt, so that after 10 years the debts are paid off by the tax revenues. After the debts have been paid off, all taxes on assets must be abolished again.

5.5 Tax account[39]

Every citizen of age of majority and every company active inland must have at least one account with the People's Bank, namely the tax account. The tax number corresponds to the People's Bank tax account number. Every citizen and every company can see the amount of taxes paid per year on their tax account. In the tax game before the budget vote, citizens and all employees of a company can distribute these taxes.

The booking procedures run automatically. Every bank that works inland or has naturalised persons or companies as customers is obliged to set up tax diversions. The amounts are first booked to the tax account and, after tax deduction, immediately transferred to the account of the specified bank.

Separate accounts are instituted for citizens and companies in order to be able to tax consumption or production separately. In the event of double taxation, the tax account holder can track each tax transaction and, in case of doubt, file a report with the People's Bank for suspected double taxation.

If a municipality administers at least the Ministry of Finance itself on a municipal basis after a subsidiarity vote[40] , the entries via the tax accounts of affected citizens are redirected accordingly.

39§153,1,2 Exclusion of double taxation: BV Art.134
40Ministry of State Organisation - 10.3 Subsidiarity vote

5.5.1 VAT account

Citizens can have their accounts at the People's Bank or at other banks, but they must at least have the tax account at the People's Bank. The tax account serves as a VAT account for them. All account outflows through transfers or cash withdrawals from the current account are diverted via the VAT account. The VAT rate is deducted there and the remaining amount is then forwarded to the specified bank account or the ATM used.

5.5.2 Company tax account

Companies can have their accounts at People's Bank or another bank, but they must at least have their tax account at People's Bank. Citizens who earn money only from employment with a company do not need their own company account. The tax account serves as a company tax account.

For sales tax, all inflows to the company account are diverted through the company tax account where the sales tax is deducted and then the balance is transferred to the company account.

For profit tax, all inflows and outflows of the company account are diverted, recorded and forwarded through the company tax account. At the end of each month, the outflows are deducted from the inflows. If there is a surplus, the profit tax is deducted from this amount and posted by direct debit from the company account to the company tax account. After this process, account withdrawals may be made once a month to the owners, the amount of which they determine themselves. However, profit withdrawals may not bring the company account into the red.

5.6 Tax Directory

In the Tax Directory, each taxpayer is given a profile showing how much tax they have paid, the average number of taxes paid per capita and the total number of taxes paid. In groups, So-called tax classes, the taxes for added value, companies, fees and tariffs are listed. For the change of economic form, the tax classes are broken down by economic form in which they were paid. In the annual budget vote, the tax amount is distributed by the people to the ministries. Each individual taxpayer can distribute his or her paid taxes in the tax game.

5.7 Company Auditing Agency tax auditor[41]

The tax auditors examine the revenues and expenditures of companies and ministries.[42] They work with the Audit Court and the Tax Office to audit ministries. Tax auditors are employees of the Company Auditing Agency and work in the field service in companies and ministries. They follow the laws of the ministries of finance, economy, labour and state organisation when auditing.

They check the economic data of the companies and ministries for tax evasion or tax fraud, secure evidence and hand the case over to the Tax Investigation Department.[43] The penalties are regulated by the Ministry of Justice in the Criminal Tax Code.[44] All data collected from ministries must be published immediately via the intranet and at the latest by the time of the budget vote on Government Television .[45]

5.8 Tax reduction[46]

State revenues are distributed separately, so that taxes become more like fees, to be used for specific purposes. This creates a more direct responsibility for profit or loss economies, which can be more easily attributed by voters to the responsible ministry. In the tax game, citizens are allowed to distribute their self-paid levies through the People's Computer itself. The budget vote continues to determine how state revenues are spent in the long run.

41 §148,7 Principles of taxation: BV Art.104, §158,2,3 Finances of ministries: BV Art.183
42 Ministry of Labour - 20.7.1 Tax auditor
43 Ministry of Security - 8.3 Tax Investigation Department
44 Ministry of Justice - 8.5.1 Taxes
45 Ministry of Media - 7 Government Television
46 §154,1,2,3 Tax reduction

The reduction in taxes envisages having to levy fewer taxes in the medium term and none at all in the long term, unless the management function of the economic ratios cannot be fulfilled either by laws or by monetary and currency policy of the central and Note-issuing Banks. In the medium term, the value added tax should be sufficient to finance all state services. In the long term, all profits of the ministries should be sufficient to finance all state services, except the Unconditional Basic Income.

The state, through its ministries, becomes entrepreneurial by being a service provider to the people. State expenditure is to be covered by fees and profits from assets and state enterprises. Wherever possible, a state service shall be financed by a fee and not by taxes. A 10% profit surcharge shall be levied on fees. Savings of the state are invested profitably by the People's Bank. People's Innovation Companies pay a dividend on their shares, some of which belong to the Ministry of Finance.

All these revenues flow into the state budget, which is used to finance services that are not chargeable, for example because this would disadvantage individuals or promote social inequality. This is decided by the people in the budget vote.

In the long term, all state services, except those of the Ministry of Education and Democratic Participation through the Ministry of State Organisation, Media and Digital Affairs, are to be bound by cost-covering fees including 10% profits. These profits are to partially cover the expenses of the exempted ministries. For the rest of the expenses, the People's Innovation Companies earn monopoly profits on the international market with the patented products. The permanent start-up of People's Innovation Companies by the Ministry of Innovation is to compensate for profit losses due to expiring patents or copied products. People's Innovation Companies are only to operate as long as they can generate monopoly profits. If profits fall by 25% due to other companies on the international market that reduce sales as competitors, the People's Innovation Company is sold to the highest bidder or transferred to the employees by employee decision.[47]

---

47 Ministry of Innovation - 10.6 Privatisation

6 Unconditional Basic Income[48]

Unconditional Basic Income is an income paid to all nationals of age of majority on the 15th day of the month. Everyone receives the same amount per capita. The payment is made to the current account of the citizen's account at the People's Bank.

The Unconditional Basic Income is made up of a share of business taxes and the income from the Unconditional Basic Income Fund. The Unconditional Basic Income thus fluctuates according to the economic performance and the degree of automation. At the beginning, the Unconditional Basic Income is low and starts as soon as an amount of 100 euros can be paid out.

The more automation advances, the higher the Unconditional Basic Income rises. As soon as automation has progressed to such an extent that 80% of the Gross Domestic Product is generated by machines, the machine fee is abolished. However, the Unconditional Basic Income fund then only distributes 80% of its returns annually and pays the rest into the Unconditional Basic Income fund in order to benefit from the compound interest effect. The fund management no longer invests exclusively in automation, but in People's Bank's most profitable and safest financial products.

Of all the business tax rates of the economic forms, the same proportion is used for Unconditional Basic Income. At the beginning it is 0.5%. The share of business taxes increases as ministries of economy switch their Tax-funded services to fees and build up their own savings.

The business taxes remain the same and thus increase the Unconditional Basic Income. Unconditional Basic Income then increases and decreases with business taxes and the economic situation of the economic forms. In addition, the income from the Unconditional Basic Income fund remains and secures a basic amount of Unconditional Basic Income. The basic amount is to be set at a level that can ensure survival in the market economy at the standard of basic supply of the Planned Economy.

How much business taxes should be reduced and how high

48§154.5 Tax reduction

the Unconditional Basic Income should be is decided by the people in a committee.

6.1 Machine fees

The machinery fees are part of the business taxes. While the business taxes finance the state services for the companies and are determined by the ministries of economy, the machine fees are earmarked and are collected by the Ministry of Finance. Machine fees finance automation on the one hand and Unconditional Basic Income on the other. They amount to 50% of the savings from using machine labour instead of human labour. 50% of the income from the machine fees is paid into the Automation Fund and 50% into the Unconditional Basic Income Fund.

6.1.1 Calculation of the machine fee

The machine charge applies whenever machines replace a human job in whole or in part. The Company Auditing Agency's economic auditors are responsible for the calculations. The calculations determine what savings result from the introduction of machine labour. The cost of machine labour is subtracted from the cost of human labour. This gives the savings for the company in switching to machine labour. The savings must be positive, otherwise the company would not automate its production. From these savings, 50% is deducted as the machine fee. As soon as the conversion to machine labour has generated the purchase price of the machine, the machine fee is incurred.

As a data basis, the economic auditors use the data of the entrepreneur and all comparable companies that have arisen in the past 5 business years. If no data is available for the machines, the data sheets and cost estimates from the machine manufacturers are used and the use is simulated for 5 years.

6.1.1.1 Human labour costs

All costs incurred in the company for the employees who were replaced by the machines are added up. This includes wages, holidays and average sick days in a year. In most cases, jobs are not replaced entirely, but all jobs are increasingly automated until no human is needed at all, or a machine can no longer replace a human. For all these pro-rata calculations, more detailed examinations become necessary.

The Company Auditing Agency's economic auditors determine in their audits how many human working hours are saved and what the hourly wage of that worker was when the machine was not in use. If labour services are paid and not working hours, the economic auditors calculate the price of the human services that were taken over by the machine. The calculations are based on the amount of wages and the amount of work. At the end of the calculation, it is clear what the cost of human labour is in relation to the good or service produced.

6.1.1.2 Costs for machine work

In addition to the costs for employees, the costs for the machine are also calculated. This includes the running costs for operation, maintenance and repair. The acquisition costs are not included because the machine fee is only incurred once the savings have recovered the acquisition costs. As soon as a machine is newly acquired, its costs are covered by the automation fund and are not included in the calculation of the machine fee. At the end of the calculation, it is clear what the cost of machine labour is in relation to the good or service produced. If machines do more in less time, this reduces the cost per unit compared to human labour.

6.1.2 Automation fund

The automation fund is used to purchase machines and convert production processes to more machine work. In general, every company is entitled to the payment of its deposits from the machine fee in order to invest them in automation. For this to happen, the amount paid in must first reach the necessary level to be able to cover the investment sum. Proportional use is also possible if the entrepreneurs wish to use additional equity or debt capital. The innovation auditors are responsible for auditing the expenditure on automation taken from the fund and, if necessary, advising the entrepreneurs.

It is crucial that the saved amounts of the automation fund are invested on an ongoing basis in order to generate returns. The People's Bank investment department is responsible for the investments. This return flows into a separate pot of the automation fund. The Ministry of Innovation can use it to promote automation that is in line with its innovation policy. First and foremost, state services are automated.

6.1.3 Funds of the Unconditional Basic Income

The Unconditional Basic Income fund is initially saved only and nothing is distributed. The savings of the fund are invested in shares and bonds of companies involved in the production of automation machines. As soon as the return from shares and bonds has reached a level where 100 euros can be paid to each nationals each month, the distribution begins.

Increasing automation increases the payments into the fund and thus the amount that can be invested and consequently the revenues from the returns. The returns are also paid into the fund to be saved there over a year. At the end of the year, the total returns are added up and divided by 12. This results in the monthly amount of Unconditional Basic Income that is paid out in the coming year.

7 Budget consolidation[49]

Fiscal consolidation refers to a balanced budget or a budget in surplus. In the state there are municipalities, the nation and the four economic forms. The national Ministry of Finance administers the budget of the entire state. As such, it is responsible for ensuring that revenues are complete and on time based on applicable laws and that expenditures are

---

49§161,1,2,3 Financial and burden equalisation: BV Art. 135

allocated to ministries based on past budget votes.

Should municipalities have decided in a subsidiarity vote[50] to administer at least the Ministry of Finance themselves, the affected Ministry of Finance of the municipality assumes responsibility. This municipality will not be involved in the national financial and burden equalisation.

The national Ministry of Finance audits the revenues and expenditures of all municipalities and economic forms. As a general rule, the revenues and expenditures of each municipality and economic form should be balanced or may have surpluses. Before the budget vote, the Ministry of Finance publishes the revenues and expenditures of the past financial year. The citizens can see the revenues and expenditures of all municipalities and economic forms and decide where to save or invest.

Normally, national ministers are responsible for fulfilling state responsibilities throughout the country. Their municipal deputies adapt the tasks to the local circumstances. There may be differences in revenues and expenditures, but these are structurally intentional because localities complement each other and balance their finances in exchange. These policy deciders are up to the politicians. The Ministry of Finance may only intervene in these decisions if this disadvantages other ministries, municipalities or economic forms. The ministers have the task of ensuring that the differences in financial productivity between the municipalities are small. All economic ministers ensure that each economic form is financially productive enough not to be dependent on subsidies but to complement each other through their economic cycles.

7.1 Financial and burden equalisation

In principle, municipalities and economic forms carry out a financial and burden equalisation. This means that municipalities and economic forms that earn surpluses must spend these surpluses to compensate for losses incurred by other municipalities and economic forms. These equalisation payments are linked to binding measures for the loss-making

50 Ministry of State Organisation - 10.3 Subsidiarity vote

municipalities or economic forms if the people do not want to tolerate these equalisation payments in the long term. Which measure is to be used is decided at the budget vote.

First, the loss-making municipality or economic form can be obliged to cope with the same revenues as all other regions. In return, the state revenues are distributed equally per capita. Every citizen then receives the same amount. The more citizens live in a municipality or economic form, the more state revenues flow there. Second, loss-making municipalities and economic forms can be forced to reduce their expenditures by cutting or eliminating state services. Thirdly, they can be forced to invest in the self-sufficiency of their inhabitants or entrepreneurs in order to reduce state services.

In order for municipalities and economic forms to have financial leeway to help themselves, they are allowed to keep and administer 10% of their revenues from profits themselves each year.

The economic form of the Free Market Economy occupies a special position. As long as anarchy prevails internationally and there is no world state, the Free Market Economy is in international competition for low wages and taxes. Therefore, the Free Market Economy must use all surpluses to reduce taxes. In return, it receives no subsidies when it makes losses. The only exception is the compensation payments when the Free Market Economy has the unemployed and impoverished pensioners supported by the Planned Economy.[51]

7.1.1 Regional specifics

Should a region have geographical or socio-demographic characteristics that lead to losses, the Ministry of Finance can summon all affected ministers and their deputies from the affected regions to a committee. In this committee, solutions are to be found together with the affected citizens. This is usually connected with structural aid through investments that are intended to improve the condition permanently.

An example of a geographical feature is mountain regions that limit mobility. One solution would be to look at

51 Ministry of Labour - 9.7 Balancing the economic forms

successful mountain regions in the world and try to make the infrastructure and business ideas similar. This could, for example, be connected to the construction of mountain railways or pumped-storage power stations.

An example of a socio-demographic feature are regions where the population is ageing because ageing humans stay and younger humans move away. Utilities for older humans may suffer shortages because there are no staff to support them, but they themselves are retired and no longer working. Care facilities for young humans, such as schools, would suffer losses because the expenditure per pupil is not sufficient to cover the costs of buildings and teachers. One solution would be to let the elderly support themselves by forming Residential Communities, carpools and shopping communities. Schools could become multi-purpose buildings and teachers could become multi-purpose employees who also take on other state service jobs.

These examples show that for each individual case, policy solutions are needed with which the local population agrees and which they come up with themselves if possible.

7.2 Savings deposits

The Ministry of Finance is obliged to save, because only the assets saved from the revenues may be used in the next budget year. Planning a budget with new debts is not permitted. In addition, savings are built up for economic downturns and reforms. Any expenditure over and above the current cost of services provided by ministries is a special request and is subject to an extra vote in the budget vote. If the revenues of the previous year are not sufficient, the savings have to be used up to pay for the special requests. Such special requests must be allocated by auctioning the savings.

7.2.1 Compound interest

The state may only borrow in exceptional cases and with the consent of the people. The state is supposed to save money to make investments. Every ministry that receives its annual budget is allowed to save if the purpose was already clear in the budget vote, for example for a new road. Compound interest causes the saved assets to increase faster than when borrowed assets are repaid, because the compound interest effect is missing there. This means that repaying a loan takes longer than saving. Exceptions are, first, loans for investments that reduce state service costs, above the compound interest effect. Secondly, loans can be taken out for the start-up capital of state enterprises that are able to generate revenues with which loans can be repaid faster than money can be saved.

7.3 Debt conversion

If it has become necessary for the state to borrow abroad, these debts must be repaid as a matter of priority. The short-term debt conversion is done by using bank balances of the current and call money accounts of nationals at the People's Bank. If these assets are not sufficient, government bonds must be sold to nationals, banks or insurance companies as soon as possible. The aim should be that interest payments on government bonds strengthen purchasing power inland and not abroad. Once all foreign debts have been repaid, the debt conversion is complete.

7.4 Debt reduction

All debts must be reduced as quickly as possible. For this purpose, the Ministry of Finance develops annual plans together with the population. The maximum number of years for debt reduction is determined by the duration of the government bonds issued. Accordingly, ten-year government bonds can be debt reduced in a ten-year plan.
The Ministry of Finance convenes a committee in which it submits proposals to the people. The citizens then choose

proposals and can adapt them to their needs. Depending on how high the debts are or how quickly they are to be repaid, several proposals can be implemented at the same time. The aim of all proposals must be neither to reduce consumption nor investment, which would be a hindrance. It is important that all measures do not encourage citizens to consume less or companies to postpone investments. Citizens can also draft their own proposals for debt reduction and put them to the initial vote. The Ministry of Finance offers debt reduction options and the people can choose one or more options in a voting.

After one year, a further People's Committee takes stock and determines how well the measures applied have worked. Based on these evaluations, it can be estimated how many years the measures would have to be continued until the state is debt-free. The people can come up with further ideas on how savings could be made without affecting consumption or investment. During the debt reduction, the people have to do more, work longer or faster and do honorary service. The people should make proposals and comment on how long they are willing to work under these strenuous conditions. For example, there could also be high-powered intervals of one week per quarter over 10 years. The point is to tell the population a period of time when the high performance phase starts and how often one has to have such a phase until the state is debt-free. The people must know when the debt reduction will be completed, because this state of affairs cannot be expected of any human being in the long run. Various calculation models are presented to the people, on the basis of which the people can decide in votes.

7.4.1 Debt reduction options

Higher taxes manage to slow down the growth of Gross Domestic Product to zero. The business tax and the value added tax are increased in proportion to the growth of the Gross Domestic Product, so that the Gross Domestic Product remains the same. These taxes are used for debt reduction.

Through voluntary work during holiday and holiday

periods, citizens can participate in construction work for state construction projects or People's Innovation Company free of charge. Disaster management provides food and accommodation and charges a fee to cover the costs. After work, there is a camp atmosphere with sponsored barbecue, beer, campfire and live music.

Due to a stagnation of real wages, companies receive more profits, which they have to pay to the Ministry of Finance. Collective bargaining autonomy is suspended and wages increase each quarter only by the measured inflation rate of the previous quarter. Companies that pay wages have to transfer the wage difference between the inflation rate and the growth of the Gross Domestic Product to the Ministry of Finance. For example, €1000 becomes €1010 in wages after a quarter with 1% inflation. But if there was 2% Gross Domestic Product growth, it should have been 1020€ wage. So companies pay 10€ per wage earner to the Ministry of Finance.

Fewer holidays will increase economic output. The number of holiday days will be halved at most for all citizens, so that no loss of the tourism industry is to be expected. If possible, holidays should only be taken inland during debt reduction in order to support the domestic economy. Companies that have to pay for fewer holiday days save costs and can charge for services rendered during this time, which in turn increases turnover. The increased profits must be paid to the Ministry of Finance.

Unpaid overtime increases economic output. The number of hours per week is increased, but the wage remains the same. The companies' additional profits from this extra work flow to the Ministry of Finance.

Taxes on assets are used to tax inheritances, gifts and annually land, which reduces purchasing power. This measure is mainly used to reduce the debt of future generations when the current generation has lived beyond its means.

7.5 Balancing the business cycles[52]

The Ministry of Finance operates a fund that is used to offset economic fluctuations. Economic fluctuations mean inflation or unemployment, which can be self-reinforcing and thus increase the fluctuation band, which can cause considerable damage to the people. The Ministry of Finance sets a maximum permissible fluctuation band of 5% inflation and 5% unemployment.

If at least one economic form moves out of range, the Ministry of Finance intervenes. Should one economic form experience a strong and sustained upswing or downswing, the Ministry of Finance coordinates action between all four ministries of economy. Should the fluctuations spread to several economic forms or to the whole country, the Ministry of Finance can, if necessary, intervene in the autonomy of the ministries of economy. All interventions are coordinated with the people and can influence the monetary and fiscal policy of one or more ministries of economy, regulate foreign trade or determine the budget management of the affected ministry of economy. Companies can be obliged to accumulate reserves in phases of upswing, which they have to use again in phases of downswing. If possible, the interventions are only made in the economic form that caused the escalating fluctuations. They are to be discontinued as soon as the economic development is again within the permissible range of fluctuation.

7.5.1 Business Cycle Compensation Fund

To ensure that the Ministry of Finance has sufficient financial leeway for economic aid during economic crises, it creates the Business Cycle Adjustment Fund. The fund is designed to reduce fluctuations by itself. This fund is an account of the Ministry of Finance at the People's Bank. Here, 30% of the additional tax revenues are deposited that arise when the Gross Domestic Product increases within a year. If the Gross Domestic Product decreases, taxes are managed down. The

---

[52]§213,1-3,5,6 Economic policy: BV Art. 100, §157,4 Budget management: KV Art.101

tax cut depends on the decline in Gross Domestic Product in the previous year. An investment tax can have an additional braking effect in phases of upswing and create reserves that can be invested in the coming phase of downturn. The aim should be to build up reserves from additional tax revenues in phases of the upswing for phases of the downswing of the business cycles. The maximum amount of the reserves saved in the fund should be 10% of the Gross Domestic Product, so that even strong downturns or slight downturns can be compensated for over several years. This will weaken the swings of the business cycles and bring them closer to the arithmetic mean.

8 State revenues[53]

The state receives its revenues from taxes, fees, assets, profits and, in case of need, also through debts. State revenues are booked at the People's Bank to the accounts of those ministries that generated the revenues. Some revenues are earmarked, others are fixed by law and some depend on economic success. Some revenues flow directly to the ministries and their employees, others are saved for the national budget of the coming year.

8.1 Taxes

Tax revenues are not earmarked and flow into the national budget for the coming year. Revenues from taxes come from value added tax, business taxes and tariffs. All taxes paid in kind either replace costs or are sold. Value added tax is considered a source of revenue on the one hand, and for the management of consumption of goods and services in the economy on the other, because it can make consumption more expensive or cheaper. Business tax is an instrument of the respective economic forms and taxes turnover or profits. Through it, the state receives revenues and can manage production by making it more expensive through higher taxes and vice versa. Business taxes can be partially or fully earmarked for Unconditional Basic Income if the economy is sufficiently automated. Tariffs, in turn, manage foreign trade and can make it more expensive

---

53§146 Procurement of funds: KV Art.102

or cheaper. They serve as a source of revenue to replace the loss of value added tax through foreign trade. As soon as states unify, tariffs are eliminated and replaced by the common value added tax.

Taxes on assets are an instrument to manage debt in such a way that the generation that created the guilt is burdened with it. This tax is independent of the economic forms. It applies to inheritances, gifts and annually to land.

Taxes are managed by the Ministry of Finance through the tax accounts at the People's Bank. If municipalities wish to levy additional taxes, they receive their additional tax money in full immediately from the Ministry of Finance.

8.2 Fees[54]

All state services paid directly or by subscription are fees. Unlike tax, they are earmarked for a specific purpose. Their price consists of the costs incurred plus a 10% profit mark-up. The fees ensure entrepreneurial activity in the authorities that provide the services. For consumers, the fees represent market prices that are not excessive. Thanks to the profit mark-up, other state expenditures that are not eligible for fees can also be covered. Fees should under no circumstances be so low that they have to be tax-subsidised. Exceptions are to be regulated in the law. Royalties are awarded for inventions made in state institutes, education and research institutions. The innovation auditors market these licences to suitable companies.

8.3 Assets

The state saves assets that are available in the upcoming budget vote. Saving amounts are granted as overdraft facilities to People's Bank customers or invested in People's Bank financial products until the budget vote. The interest rates for overdraft facilities are 10%.

Wealth accumulation goes through three phases. In the first phase, the national budget of one year is saved. The amount

---

54§157.2 Budget management

saved is considered to have been reached as soon as it is equal to the expenditure of the previous financial year. In the second phase, the Gross Domestic Product of a year is saved. As soon as the savings amount has reached the amount of the Gross Domestic Product of the previous year, the savings target is considered to have been met. In the third and final phase, all revenues exceeding the Gross Domestic Product of the previous year are to be used to reduce the value added tax. First, the value added tax on basic foodstuffs will be phased out. The assets above the state budget will be invested more long-term. Specialists from the People's Bank's investment department will take care of this.

8.4 Profits[55]

The state generates profits through its authorities and operations. For every euro spent, between 1.02 and 1.1 euros flow back to the state. This margin of 2 to 10% gives the ministries leeway to adjust to the economy. The 10% ceiling can also be changed in voting with the people, but the constitution must be amended to do so. The profit margin is the amount covered by the costs plus 10% of these costs. Exceptions apply to People's Innovation Company. The revenues from the profits go 25% to the ministry, 25% to the employees of the affected ministry and 50% to the national budget. The amount paid to the employees is based on their work performance. Thus, the most hard-working employees get the highest profit-sharing and the slowest employee gets no profit-sharing at all.[56] The amount that goes to the ministry can be used in the spirit of the ministry. In the ministry's interest are investments in the ministry's infrastructure and service delivery, compensation for additional costs beyond the amount of the budget vote, or saving for future costly projects. The amount that goes into the national budget can be distributed by the citizens in the budget vote. The amount earmarked for the budget vote remains in the ministry's

55§147 Profits of ministries, §157,1,2 Budget management: BV Art. 126, §213,4 Economic policy: BV Art. 100
56Ministry of Labour - 4.8.2 Bonus-malus system

account until the budget vote, but can be invested through the People's Bank's investment department, further increasing profits. The people can expropriate the savings and profits of the ministries and allocate them entirely to the national budget in the course of the budget vote.

In the long term, the profits should contribute to reducing taxes.

8.4.1 Offices and authorities

Offices and authorities provide services or goods to citizens. These products are subject to fees and are priced publicly. In the Social Market Economy or Planned Economy, most state services are offered as compulsory insurance or as a subscription, which is paid together with the business tax. Those who do not have a subscription pay for the services individually.

8.4.2 Natural monopolies

Natural monopolies are companies that provide a service that involves very high initial investment, but then have low running costs. As an example, consider a power plant that produces electricity. It is very expensive to build, but afterwards each additional customer costs very little. It is the same with roads, data networks or sewage systems.

These natural monopolies have the property that the total cost of providing a good is significantly lower when only one company, rather than several competing companies, provides the service. This saving is appropriated by the people, as the infrastructure to support the population is only provided by state-owned companies. The second saving in contrast to natural monopolies in market economy management is the lower price. Once the high initial investment has been recovered, the price can be greatly reduced. A market economy monopolist would keep prices high because customers desperately need these services and there is no substitute. Natural monopolies in state hands, on the other hand, are interested in increasing the common good.

The fees therefore finance maintenance and technological renewal. A 10% profit is added to this amount. This profit margin is small for monopolies, but these natural monopolies belong to the citizens and thus at the same time to the consumers.

8.4.3 People's Innovation Company

People's Innovation Companies belong to the people and only produce products that enjoy patent protection. These companies are monopolists in the market for the time that the patent protection is valid. They can therefore charge monopoly prices for the products. Nationals and companies in the Social Market Economy receive discounts of around 40%. The rest of the consumers pay the monopoly price.

The profits are first used to repay the debts incurred by the People's Bank through the construction of the People's Innovation Company. Then the profits of the People's Innovation Company will be distributed.[57]

8.5 Debts[58]

Debts are revenues that the state may only incur as an exception and with the consent of the people. Exceptions apply in emergency situations, in which case the voting must take place within 3 months. Other exceptions are reforms and investments. Debts may only be used for reforms that make the state system more favourable or worthwhile. This means that at the time the debt is taken out, it must be clear by when this amount will have been saved through the new efficiency. Debts for investments in new People's Innovation Companies of the Ministry of Innovation or major construction projects of individual ministries may be taken on if they have passed the economic auditor's efficiency test and the rating agency

---

57 Ministry of Innovation - 10.4.6 Distribution of profits
58 §157.3 Budget management

gives them a high repayment capacity rating.[59]

The state incurs debts by issuing government bonds. They are issued only through the People's Bank and only to nationals. This is to avoid capital export through interest payments abroad. Bonds have a maturity of between 6 months and 10 years. The amounts in the People's Bank's current and call money accounts can be used as short-term debts, So-called bridging loans. The minimum reserve ratio is 5% and unlimited deposit insurance applies. Only in the case of deposit insurance, i.e. if too many citizens withdraw their credit balances from the People's Bank accounts, may debts be taken out on the international financial market.

The debt ceiling is set by the amount of money in People's Bank current and call money accounts and is published annually. The interest rate for bridging loans corresponds to the growth rate of the Gross Domestic Product in the previous quarter. If growth was negative, the interest rate remains at 0%. If the state withdraws money from the current and call money accounts of citizens and companies, the interest payment is due at the end of a month until the amount has been reimbursed.

The special termination right allows account holders to dispose of their full account balance at any time. The minimum reserve is used for this purpose and the missing amount is rescheduled. The debt conversion works in the same way as taking out debt. All People's Bank current and call money accounts are debited at the same percentage needed to cover the demand. In this way, each account holder receives the same share of the interest rate. If an account holder needs part or all of the amount borrowed, he no longer receives interest and the other current and call money accounts are charged more accordingly.

8.6 Increase money supply

Innovations, such as new roads and pipelines, can be paid for with newly printed money if they create added value. For implementation, the affected ministry that wants to introduce

---

59 Ministry of Labour - 20.7.3 Economic auditor, 18.4 Rating agency

the innovations must find a majority in the budget vote. Then the Central Bank is allowed to issue the corresponding amount of money. Depending on the currency in which the benefits are paid, the Note-issuing Bank affected must disburse the necessary amount of money to the ministry concerned.

For example, a new road is created with new kinds of machines that build a better road in less time. Both savings represent added value that does not lead to the devaluation of the currency when it is printed. A new road with a surface that lets water through, reduces noise and generates electricity adds value through environmental protection, fewer repairs, healthier residents and revenues from electricity sales. New pipes carry more and more diverse things, which means new revenues can be collected for transport. Empty conduits allow additional new things to be added to lines easily and cheaply. This results in savings in the future. All these new revenues and savings form an added value that is anticipated in the newly spent money supply. The newly issued money supply must not exceed these surplus values in order to avoid inflation or a devaluation of the currency.

8.7 Principles for the distribution of state revenues[60]

State expenditure is determined in the budget vote. The ministries receive their monetary amounts at the beginning of the new financial year. This should enable the ministries to fulfil their state tasks in a way that meets the needs of the people and the region and is economically economical or profitable. In order to be able to fulfil the social rights granted in the constitution, the expenditure for basic supply services is financed by tax revenue if necessary. The polity consists of all ministries and is divided into the municipal, national and international political levels under federalism. The costs incurred for state services are borne by the affected ministry, regardless of the political level at which they are incurred. However, the benefits from the services can be distributed differently between the political levels. Accordingly, in the budget vote, the costs are broken down by benefit at the

60§156 Principles for the allocation of tax funds: BV Art. 43a municipal, national or international level to narrow down those entitled to vote. The basic rule is that whoever derives the benefit from a service also bears the cost. At the same time, the bearer of the costs is allowed to determine the benefit. At the state level, citizens manage the costs through their taxes. Since, under state law, the ministries are the property of the citizens, costs can also be borne through profits made by the ministries. The citizens receive proposals from the ministries as to how the service should be designed and what costs it will incur. In the budget vote, the citizens then decide how much money from state revenues should be spent on which services as state expenditure.

For example, a power plant in a municipality may generate costs for construction and operation, but provides a benefit to the nation by distributing the energy nationwide. In this case, the nation bears the costs. The people vote on construction and operation as part of the budget vote. If, on the other hand, a city hall is built in a municipality, for example, only the citizens of the municipality benefit. The municipality must have generated sufficient state revenues to finance the construction and operation of the city hall. The citizens of the municipality must approve the financing in the budget vote and may determine the use of the municipal hall.

9 State expenditure[61]

All state expenditure is summarised in the budget. The budget is prepared annually and must be voted on by the people before it can be spent according to plan in the new financial year. A financial year runs from the first of July to the thirtieth of June.

The budget is saved over a year and may also include other savings built up over previous years. It is managed economically so that revenues exceed expenditures. The originators of expenditure must first solicit the revenues for that expenditure through the budget vote. In the event of economic fluctuations, the budget can be reduced or expanded. The Ministry of Finance is responsible for bringing together all revenues earmarked for the state budget, as well as for bringing together all ministry

61 §157,4-8 Budget management: KV Art.101, §84,4 Political civil rights

financial plans earmarked for the draft budget. New ministry tasks must first reach the cost-covering amount in an auction during the budget vote in order to receive their funding basis. New tasks that the ministries wish to finance with their own savings from profits are exempt from this.

In the course of the annual budget vote, all expenditures are reviewed for their necessity and appropriateness. Only if the financial impact is acceptable to the population will they vote for it by majority.

If, in the course of the year, higher expenditures are made than voted, these expenditures must be stopped immediately. If this is not possible, the savings of the originating ministry are used. If this is not sufficient, the current savings for the next year's budget are tapped. Ministers who live beyond their means through their own fault are liable for this with their office. If a criminal offence can be linked to the excessive state expenditure, ministers are also liable with their private assets. To avoid this, a committee can be convened to draw up a supplementary budget, which can then be voted on.

9.1 Financial plans of the ministries[62]

Each ministry prepares its own budget in cooperation with its workers. This process is repeated annually and ends 2 months before the budget vote. It lists all current costs for real estate, equipment, material and personnel that are necessary for the state services of the coming year. Using the Algoracle[63] , simulations are made of probabilities of how the population will develop in the coming year and how state services will be demanded to varying degrees. State services must always have a legal basis and can therefore be easily defined as recurring expenditures. This part of the financial plan is headed "basic amount".

The situation is different with new tasks, reforms or projects, which may cause one-time higher and, in addition, further ongoing expenses. The financial plan describes the planned

62 §213,4 Economic policy: BV Art. 100, §158,1,2 Finances of ministries: BV Art.183
63 Ministry of Digital Affairs - 15.3 Algoracle

reforms and projects and provides binding cost estimates.

In their planning, the ministries take into account the overall economic situation in all economic forms and adjust their revenues and expenditures. In phases of economic downturn, state revenues are reduced and expenditures are increased. In phases of upswing, it is the other way round.

The individual costs are presented as a picture, text or video. The price is mentioned and whether the costs are to be financed through savings of the ministry or through the budget.

Each ministry also reports in its financial plan the expenditure incurred in the past financial year, from which estimates for future expenditure are derived. Expenditure for all law services and projects, such as salaries, operating costs, uses of profits and reform costs, is recorded. Insofar as a cost-covering fee plus 10% profit margin is charged for a service, this cost factor is also reported, but marked as Fee-funded.

Reform costs are costs for the new construction, reconstruction, expansion or dismantling of a service or ministry. The uses for the profits earned by the ministry in the past year indicate how the 25% of the profits that the ministry itself is allowed to distribute were distributed. Operating costs consist of materials and supplies of all services provided by the government and are sorted by ministry and postcode area. Salaries are all wages of all ministers, politicians and other state employees and are also sorted by ministry and postcode area.

A description of the service is provided in the listing. The services to be provided are described, as well as the number of citizens who will benefit from the service and the price that the service will cost in total and per capita of users, citizens or people.

Example traffic:

In Euro	Village road	Highway
User	50 users for 25 years	1 000 000 000 users for 15years
Construction project costs	10 000 € Redevelopment	500 000 000 € New building
Running costs	1000 € per year Sweeping, removing vegetation, repairing	10 000 000 € per year Repair
Salaries	Mayor, 48 000 € per year Road maintenance 24 000 € per employee per year	Minister of Infrastructure, 90 000 € per year Infrastructure construction group 30 000 € per employee per year Company Auditing Agency 50 000 € per employee per year

9.1.1 Visualisation on the intranet[64]

All ministries publish their current and planned revenues and expenditures for the coming year on their intranet profile pages in the State Directory. Via a menu, each ministry can be shown individually where it provides services on the domestic map. This information is further subdivided into nation and municipality, as well as into current services and new projects. The audit report of the Company Auditing Agency[65] and the simulation from the Algoracle[66] are stored with each entry. For ongoing services, the affected laws[67] and a video of the service in the Party Television media library[68] are also linked.

---

64 §155.4 State expenditure: BV Art. 167
65 Ministry of Labour - 20.8.8 Audit report
66 Ministry of Digital Affairs - 15.3 Algoracle
67 Ministry of Justice - 4.7 Law Directory
68 Ministry of Media Affairs - 5.6 Media Directory

9.1.2 Review of the financial plans

The Company Auditing Agency is responsible for reviewing the financial plans before they are brought together in the cabinet. The Company Auditing Agency checks new construction projects, running costs and salaries to see whether funds are being used appropriately and usefully and whether costs have been calculated adequately. With their knowledge gained from regular company audits, the staff of the Company Auditing Agency know how successful operations function or innovative projects are implemented. If there are faults or ambiguities, the draft goes back to the ministry and is newly audited.

9.2 Cabinet draft budget[69]

The Minister of Finance convenes all ministers 2 months before the budget vote to prepare the draft budget. The cabinet always meets publicly in real time on Government Television. The individual financial plans are presented and reconciled with each other. The idea here is that all ministers agree on a total amount for all state services that can be achieved with the available budget. The more that is left over from the budget, the more the citizens can still distribute to projects themselves. The ministers limit their expenditure to what is absolutely necessary. All costs that are not absolutely necessary to maintain the state enterprise are auctioned off as projects. If there are still savings of the ministry that could finance at least one reform or project, a ministry can act independently. If the citizens do not agree, there is a deselection quorum[70] of the minister and popular empowerment[71].

If the financial plans exceed the saved national budget, ministries must make a choice as to which expenditures are most important to them. In the draft budget, this is expressed in colour coding. Expenditure that is less important is shown in blue, the most important in red and moderately important in purple. The draft budget must be designed in such a way

69§155,1,2 State expenditure: BV Art. 167
70 Ministry of State Organisation - 9.5 Quorum
71 Ministry of State Organisation - 12.3 Popular empowerment

that the saved revenues are sufficient for all red expenditures. The numbers are on a coloured background, the colour of which indicates the type of revenue that will be used for it. Green stands for value added taxes, brown for tariffs, yellow for business taxes, orange for ministry profits. The medium-term goal is to reduce the share of business taxes and keep it out of the budget in the long term in order to be able to use the business tax for the Unconditional Basic Income.

9.3 Budget Committee

30 days before the budget vote, the budget committee must meet for the first time. Each ministry is given one day to discuss its expenses with the people. The budget committee then always takes place in the capital city of the respective ministry. Finally, the cabinet, i.e. all ministers, meet on the panel to finalise the budget bill. Whether the budget committee has to meet further times depends on how quickly the budget proposal is ready.

In the budget committee, the people determine what counts as the basic amount, i.e. what running costs are absolutely necessary to provide state services prescribed by law. It is not the services that are under scrutiny here, but the costs that are incurred for them. All participants in the committee are called upon to make proposals on how the service could be provided more cheaply.

The next step is to determine what new tasks, reforms or projects are. Again, the costs are reviewed, not the measures themselves. Ideas can be expressed on how the same goal can be achieved at lower cost. The choice of which measure is popular enough to be financed by the people with their budget only becomes apparent after the auction.

Participants on the panel of the Budget Committee are all 18 ministers, the leader of the Audit Court, the head of the Central Bank and the head of the Company Auditing Agency. If necessary, affected employees are also specifically invited. All participants on the panel negotiate together with the people in the audience and the spectators at the People's Computers. In the negotiations, the draft budget becomes the budget bill.

The process corresponds to the legislative process.

9.4 Election campaign

During the election campaign, ministers advertise for taxpayers' favour for their ministry's upcoming annual budget. The election campaign process takes place after the budget committee and is conducted on the basis of the budget bill. The parties finance their election campaigns through honorary service and donations. Translation and dissemination in the media of television, internet and intranet is done through the services of the Ministry of Media Affairs and the Ministry of Digital Affairs.[72] Government Television accompanies the election campaign with broadcasts on state services that are up for voting.

Election campaigns are multimedia presentations in which politicians advertise annual financial statements, major products or services, and progressive projects or reforms to curry favour with taxpayers. During the election campaign, the aim is to justify state services or rules that generate costs. The cost-benefit and cause-effect ratios must be clear to the electorate, because the people have the moral responsibility to decide how much taxpayers' money is used for what purpose.

9.4.1 State television broadcasts

Party Television[73] continuously broadcasts all filmed ministry projects co-produced with the ministry during this period. All Party Television feature films on ministry projects and all Surveillance Television reports, are linked to the media library in the Media Directory on the profile page of the People's Committee in the Committee Directory.[74]

Surveillance Television[75] continuously broadcasts all cost

---

72 Ministry of Digital Affairs - 2.1.2.1.2 Election Advertising, Ministry of Media Affairs - 2.1.1.1 Video Casting, 5.3 Advertising
73 Ministry of Media - 10 Party Television
74 Ministry of Media Affairs - 5.6 Media Directory, Ministry of State Organisation - 9.6.4 Committee Directory
75 Ministry of Media - 12 Surveillance Television

centres of the ministries during this time, showing common cost centres, such as electricity consumption by computers, as an example in one place in the ministry and displaying the total number in the ministry. The reports state the facts that unannounced investigations by a Surveillance Television monitoring team have revealed.[76] These may be spot checks, supplemented by the Company Auditing Agency's record.

In a belly band, for example, the text appears: 1000 computers in total in the administrative area of the Ministry of Labour generate electricity costs of 52,000 euros. A footnote shows the bill, which can be displayed down to the consumption in watts of each computer via links. Viewers can pause the broadcast to follow the links at their leisure and analyse the bills. The bill view automatically shows the average of all computers in kilowatts. Above the bill is what each numeral stands for.

Average con-sumption of all PCs		Period of use per day		Working days per year		Electricity price per kWh		Number of PCs in the mini-sterium	Result in €
0.13 kWatt	*	8 hours	*	250	*	0,20	*	1000	52 000

9.5 Budget vote[77]

The annual budget vote, like all elections, is held in the voting booths of the town hall, where the budget proposal is available for voting for one week. Because the ballot paper can be very extensive, voters can already edit it on their People's Computer during the election week and save this version. The voting mode in the tax game serves this purpose. In the voting booth, after logging on to the voting computer, they can then call up, control and confirm the saved version.

The distribution runs according to a direct democratic procedure in which all ministries are involved. This procedure

76Ministry of Media Affairs - 12.1 Monitoring team
77§159 budget vote, §155,3,4 state expenditure: BV Art. 167

is similar in character to the general meeting of a joint-stock company. Accordingly, the voters would be the shareholders, the politicians the managers and the Company Auditing Agency the auditors. This electoral event is also used to hold votes for laws that have come into being in the past year. This is especially true for laws that are not urgent or that result in expenditure.

The ministries compete with projects and running costs for their upcoming annual budget. In the process, the amount to be distributed is known from the beginning, because the budget is not financed with current tax revenues, but from the savings of the previous year. The money for the coming year must already be available. Accordingly, savings are made for longer for major projects. Of course, the ministries can also agree beforehand and announce a suitable amount. In the end, however, the citizens must approve the budget allocation. In this election, all projects and running costs are listed individually and can be deselected. The aim is that ministries must convince voters with their projects and with their work, year after year.

9.5.1 Ballot paper

The ballot paper is the budget bill that can be accepted, rejected or amended in whole or in part. The digital ballot paper can be unfolded more and more on the voting computer the deeper one wants to go into the individual cost centres. The voters themselves decide how many voting questions they want to answer. The budget bill at hand can be approved across the board, or all cost statements of all ministries can be rejected one by one down to the smallest cost centre in a folder structure, if everything else is approved. One can always reject or approve a superordinate folder across the board. For the voters, it is possible to obtain a further breakdown by clicking on a cost amount, so that at the end each individual cost centre is visible and this cost amount can be accepted or rejected. In case of rejection, another path opens automatically. For each path you can check [Include all lower paths]. This would be the case if one rejects a state service and all the following cost centres that are involved in this service in detail.

The ticks for consent are set by default. However, the voter can also click on "Reject" to set the tick there. For example, the folders read: Budget vote - Ministry of Security - Nation - Military - Military pay - Special task force - Military pay Captain: 40 000 euros per year [Change approval / disapproval / amount].

Basically, the ballot paper is divided into the basic amount and the project amount. It is structured like a tree, with the total amount at the bottom of the trunk, which can be accepted or rejected. The trunk is divided into the basic amount and the project amount. Each of the two trunks has 18 branches, one for each ministry. The branches of the trunks are the state services that a ministry provides in the municipality or nation. The leaves are the individual cost centres for each service. The right side of the tree structure is protected by law, namely the basic amount. The left side is auctioned off unless the project amount is large enough to fund all projects.

9.5.2 Rejections

Ministers have the opportunity to test the popularity of their services with the people through this election. However, if the rejection rate of a cost centre exceeds 75%, the cost centre is not funded and could only be financed from savings in the profits of a ministry. If the cost centre is provided for by law, a committee must be convened to advise whether the law should be amended or repealed.

Misplanning past the will of the people must be reflected in a minister's deselection quorum, not in the budget vote. By colour-coding the costs to the ministries, voters immediately know which ministers they think should be deselected. Ministers who experience a high rate of rejection of their expenses every year are thus forced to engage with the people through People's Committees to avoid being deselected. In this way, the budget vote also serves to approve the government of all ministries for the previous financial year or to open proceedings for misconduct in service or abuse of office with the help of the Audit Court.

9.5.3 Basic amount

Ministries always receive a basic amount to maintain their function. The basic amount is given in costs and uses. All expenses are already allocated. Links are given next to all state services provided for by laws. There is one link to each affected section of the law in the Law Directory, including a video of the law being filmed, and a link to a video of the Party Television where the provision of the state service was filmed. Voters can reject or approve the state service and confirm or change the cost amount.

9.5.3.1 Change costs

As soon as you change the cost amount, an input field opens. A text and an invoice can be entered in the input field to indicate how the cost amount is to be changed. Changes must be justified in terms of content and calculation, and increases must be accompanied by financing details. All proposals of this kind that have not already been made in the previous budget committee will flow into the next budget committee.

9.5.3.2 Reduce costs

If the field [too expensive] is pressed, a cost structure tree opens with all final amounts. Wherever one clicks [too expensive], the more detailed breakdown appears. Following the chain to the end, voters make a precise savings call. The ministry can respond. But if at least 10% of voters complain about too high costs at the same cost centre, they automatically trigger a review by the Company Auditing Agency, which has to prepare a status report. If the complaints rise to 50%, a committee of enquiry must be convened by the Company Auditing Agency.

9.5.3.3 Reject service

While it is possible to reject a statutory benefit, it is also equivalent to voting for the repeal quorum for the law in question. If the [Reject] box is pressed, the voter is automatically redirected to the Law Directory and the affected law or laws and can cast his or her vote for the repeal quorum there. Anyone who has cast this vote once cannot do so a second time in subsequent budget votes, unless the benefit is justified by a new law. Rejection of a benefit nevertheless remains possible in subsequent budget votes.

9.5.3.4 Distribution of business taxes[78]

Business taxes are aligned with the state services enjoyed by companies in the respective economic form. These cost centres are listed in the budget vote, but cannot be changed. If they are also protected by law, they cannot be vetoed either. Excepted from this are cost centres against which a veto quorum, repeal quorum or initiative quorum is met. They can then be negotiated in a committee to change the legal position.

In the Barter Economy, taxes are partly managed in kind. The Ministry of Barter Economy calculates which cost centres are fully or partially financed with this. In the Planned Economy, the work performed for the basic supply is listed, but cannot be rejected. A reduction in working hours to reduce costs is possible, but will result in the voter agreeing to be contacted to make an appointment to provide proof on site at the nearest Social Village. The cost of imports of materials and equipment that cannot be produced in the Planned Economy will be charged against the Planned Economy's business taxes. Only when all imports are financed can the remaining amounts be distributed in the budget vote. In the Social Market Economy, many compulsory insurances and state services are financed by subscription through the business tax. These tax revenues are considered fees and are earmarked. They cannot be rejected.

78§150.3 Business taxes

9.5.4 Project amount

The project amount is the available state budget minus the basic amount. Voters can distribute this amount of money, which is why this part of the voting is called an "auction". For all new state tasks, reforms and other projects, target amounts are given. The target amounts are the cost of the project, linked to binding cost estimates that can be viewed on the affected ministry's profile page in the State Directory. If costs appear too high to voters, they can click [too expensive], reduce the cost amount and indicate in an input field how they would reduce the cost. It is the same input field as for the basic amount to reduce costs. Rejection is expressed by allocating too little or no money to a project.

Voters can distribute the total project amount among as many projects as they wish. The count takes place at the end of the election week. The more voters have given more money to a project, the higher the project ranks. At the end of the count, all projects are funded from the most popular downwards until the entire project amount is used up. There are no projects with remaining amounts. Remaining amounts of the project amount are always saved. If the project amount in the budget proposal is already large enough to finance all projects, the auction will still take place. The last placed project does not take place and the amount is saved. Saving is a permanent project of the Ministry of Finance as long as the long-term savings target of an annual amount of Gross Domestic Product has not been reached.

If the ministries want to spend their own savings to finance a project, they must already specify the amount they would spend on it in the financial plan. This amount is deducted from the target amount.

Projects that constitute new tasks for ministries must be justified by law. If new laws are necessary, these laws must be submitted to the people for voting 37 days before the budget vote. If there is no legal basis, the project will not be included in the budget bill.

9.5.4.1 Favourite projects

Projects that do not reach their funding limit but are popular with at least 50% of the citizens are given the right to a savings pot. Annual allocations are saved in this until the funding limit has been reached. Every year, the cost of the project must be updated. If approval through tax allocation falls below 40% of the citizens, the balance from the savings pot is transferred to the state savings.

9.6 Tax game

The tax game is an intranet game that all players can play together throughout the year. People's Computer owners can access it via the intranet site of the Ministry of Finance or the Ministry of Digital Affairs under the computer games section .[79]

9.6.1 Goals

The tax game serves three purposes. First, players can distribute their paid taxes and levies to any state services they personally care about. Second, players can make it easier for themselves to fill in the ballot paper for the annual budget vote. Third, players can take their time to thoroughly research a state service, save their scores and target specific scores to import into the budget vote.

9.6.2 Levies paid

Throughout the course of the game, you have an overview of the taxes and duties you have paid so far and how much of them you have already distributed. This includes, firstly, all the value added taxes that have been deducted when transferring money from private accounts or ATMs, secondly, the business taxes, the shares of which flow into the budget, thirdly, customs duties that have accrued through consumption or production,

---

79 Ministry of Digital Affairs - 15 computer games

and fourthly, profits that have accrued to ministries because one has obtained services from them that are subject to fees. The taxes that a company earns are credited equally to the owner and each employee of the company to the account of their paid taxes in the tax game and can be distributed in the same way as other taxes. The data is newly retrieved from the People's Bank tax account of the player and his companies every time the player opens the game. It is possible to display the amounts in the currencies of the Planned Economy, Social Market Economy and Free Market Economy.

The tax game is constantly being adapted. In the medium term, more and more business taxes are to flow into the Unconditional Basic Income. Then all value added taxes, profits and tariffs will have to be distributed first, followed by business taxes.

Example:

Levy	Value added tax	Profits	Tariffs	Business tax
Euro total	2670	450	230	12565
Distributed in %	100	100	73	0

9.6.3 Distribute expenditure

With this game, you can donate the taxes you have paid to the state institutions and projects you support. Each player can decide which state services his or her taxes should go to. Should many have the same idea, it is "first come, first served." As soon as the amount necessary for financing has been reached, no more levies can be distributed there. If one feels that this cost centre should receive more money to perform better, one can overpay the amount. The overpaid amount is written next to the financed amount and deducted from the distributable taxes and levies. For each overpayment, an input field appears where players can enter what should be paid for with the extra money.

9.6.3.1 Satellite view

The management works via the three-dimensional satellite map of the inland, which is accessed via the People's Navigator[80] . One can focus into the satellite image to click on the individual cost centre. The layout resembles a computer game. To begin with, all cost centres of all domestic and communitarised[81] ministries worldwide are shown as coloured dots. Each cost item bears the colour of the ministry under whose responsibility it falls. If several ministries are involved in the costs, the round dot is shown as a pie chart. The size of the dots corresponds to the amount of money behind a cost item. Clicking on the dots shows how high the costs are and what service is provided with them.

9.6.3.2 Control bar

The control bar consists of a search bar at the top, below which is a folder structure, like in Windows Explorer, where all ministries are listed from A to Z. The search bar can be accessed via a +. Via a +, one can access the individual authorities, their organigrams and activity reports. Next to each + is the amount of money behind that folder path. At the end of a path, the monetary amount for each individual cost item is given. The cost centre searched for is displayed in full screen next to the control bar on the satellite map. The folder path corresponds to the tree structure applied to the ballot paper.

9.6.3.3 Search

Projects and institutions can now be searched, compared and selected via the left control bar. With the advanced search, one can search by postcode areas or sort ministries, sectors, offices. The results can be displayed sorted by most recent or most popular services.

---

80 Ministry of Digital Affairs - 11.4 People's Navigator
81 Ministry of Foreign Affairs - 5 Communitarisation

9.6.3.4 Presentation of the services

The state services of the past year can be displayed as text, virtual simulation or full-screen video. The text includes the legal basis for the benefits in the constitution and the laws as well as regulations and service instructions from the ministries. The virtual simulation means that the population is displayed anonymously as avatars[82] who have received the state service to be simulated in the past year. The avatars are located in the three-dimensional satellite map and receive state services, such as detention. The entire last year can be played in fast forward. The simulation game Algoracle is used for this, but this time it only evaluates data from the past and does not make any predictions for the future.

In the video, each cost centre is filmed. These videos are excerpts from filming of the tasks of all ministries by the Party Television or evidence videos of unannounced controls by the Surveillance Television. In the video, the operating hours and costs are superimposed and further details are spoken in as offtext. Employees have to say what they have done in the past year after the annual appraisal and are filmed doing so.

9.6.3.5 Updates

All costs produced by the state through its ministries are updated 3 times a year. The updates take place as soon as the Company Auditing Agency's audit report for a ministry, the financial plan of a ministry and finally the budget bill are available. The updates become increasingly important in the annual budget election campaign.

The standard game is updated as soon as the budget bill is available. All entries where the cost centres remain, as last year, can be accepted. Everything that changes this year is displayed to the player. Here he must check his entries and, if necessary, adjust them to the update.

---

82 Ministry of Digital Affairs - 11.4.4 Avatars

9.6.3.6 Rating

Citizens can tick [too expensive] or [reject] for each cost centre. When each checkmark is set, an input field opens where the reason for the decision can be given. The ministries receive the statistics of these reports from the Ministry of Digital Affairs on a weekly basis. Each player can see where and how many ticks have been set. Below that there is an input field [Amount X] where you can enter your paid levies in order to distribute them. Below the input field, the available remaining amount that can still be distributed is displayed. Before you confirm the amount, the percentage of your own levies paid in the past year that you want to distribute is displayed.

In the lower third of the side view, you can see the most popular three services that have received the most money from all players so far, as well as those that have received the least money. There are also the most recent statistics of the most expensive or rejected benefits.

9.6.4 Statistics

The voting data can also be summarised in the overall score of all players and evaluated at an early stage. The amount of tax money distributed serves the Ministers as a statistical indication of the popularity of a state service and as an argument in the negotiations in the Cabinet and the Budget Committee. All proposals made in the tax game in the input fields up to the budget committee flow into the budget committee.

The data of all participants are continuously collected by the Ministry of Digital Affairs, analysed and sent to the affected ministries. In this way, images of voters' needs are created. Politicians can see what taxes and levies should be invested in according to the citizens' will. If already more than 10% of those entitled to vote on the budget as players consider a cost centre to be too expensive, the ministry can audit the cost centre itself before the data is imported and the Company Auditing Agency does it. If the complaints rise above 50%, the ministry can examine all the players' proposals and, if necessary, work with them to implement them in order to preempt a committee of enquiry. If so many players play the game that 75% of those entitled to vote have already expressed their disapproval of a cost centre, the affected minister can convene a committee. Only in this way can he possibly avert that the cost centre is not funded.

Politicians can see which of their projects are popular and which are not. In this way, projects that are already funded in the game can start the budget vote more relaxed than those that are not. The politicians thus gain knowledge of what the citizens who participate in the game would like. The percentage of the affected population that has distributed how many taxes is displayed.

The proposals from the input fields are evaluated by the ministries and the party behind them and taken up if this proposal does not put the population at a disadvantage compared to the existing proposal. If a proposal is implemented, the proposer will be named, if he or she so wishes.

9.6.5 Import of the voting data

To make the preliminary work easier for voters, they can already distribute their tax money in the tax game. All entries are automatically taken over as soon as one has successfully logged on to the voting computer and agreed to the data retrieval. If citizens have already saved all their approvals and rejections continuously in the tax game, this data can be read out by the voting computer. To do this, the voter gives a command on his People's Computer to have a link to his data retrieved by the voting computer via the intranet. After the command, a QR code appears on the screen of the People's Computer, which must be held in front of the iris scan camera on the voting computer so that the stored completed ballot paper can be retrieved via this link. The data retrieval, like every data retrieval from the People's Computer, appears in the access log. This enables the voter to check immediately whether his or her election has been received. On the voting computer, all entries can be checked again and changed.

9.6.6 End of the game

The game ends each year with the budget vote. All levies are then set to zero and a new year begins in which levies are made that can be distributed. The default settings of the previous year can be carried over. Wherever changes were desired by [reject] or [too expensive] and current changes have occurred are displayed to the player.

9.6.7 Game variants

Apart from the standard game, where you distribute your own levies, there are two other game modes in which you can distribute all state revenues. In the "God mode", you can adjust the financial plans yourself and make a budget bill out of it. You can distribute all the revenues as you like. In "voting mode", once you have the budget bill, you can fill in the same ballot paper as on the voting computer. You can distribute all the revenues within the limits of the basic amount and the project amount. This mode is mainly used to import all the scores from the standard game and to be able to go through the ballot paper again at your leisure. A save point from this game variant can also be imported into the voting computer, which is not possible with scores in God mode.

9.7 Audit Court[83]

The Audit Court is an independent agency whose head is directly elected. The Audit Court's duties consist of auditing the state accounts, the Company Auditing Agency and all communications from citizens, especially the budget vote and tax game input boxes.

The Company Auditing Agency's audit reports for ministries and their enterprises are reviewed more frequently than those of companies and are repeated on a random basis. In particular, auditors check that state agencies comply with applicable laws

---

83§157,4 Financial management: KV Art.101, §160,1,2,3 Financial Supervisory Authority: KV Art.105, 106, §158,3 Finance of ministries: BV Art.183

and do not exceed or fall short of them. The auditors of the Audit Court have the same qualifications as the auditors of the Company Auditing Agency and have the right to conduct covert audits.

9.7.1 Data

All ministries are obliged to submit all their accounts, which they issue and which are addressed to them, to the Audit Court. On the basis of this data, the Audit Court can check the Company Auditing Agency's data, the financial plans and the draft budget. All ministries and politicians are obliged to provide the auditors of the Audit Court with full information at all times, including on secret or internal matters of the state. The auditors also have the duty to publish secret or internal matters if they can be used to prove violations of the law or waste of state property. If the auditors determine that secrecy is not actually necessary, they can report this to the head of the Audit Court, who can convene a committee. At this committee, secrecy must be justified by the affected politicians and approved by a majority of the people.

The auditors of the Audit Court must publish their audit methods as soon as the audits are completed. If it is necessary to keep audit methods secret in order to prevent manipulation, the auditors can also justify this in a committee and have the secrecy approved by the people.

9.7.2 Measures

The two sharpest weapons of the Audit Court against the waste of taxes and duties are the permanent seat on the panel of the budget committee and the veto against certain state expenditures. The Audit Court can already veto the financial plans, then again the draft budget and the budget bill. Its veto can only be broken by the people if it is overruled in the budget vote. A [veto] is marked on the ballot paper at the affected cost centres. Pressing this box brings up the Audit Court auditors' reasoning as to why that cost centre should be vetoed or the amount changed. If the voters still approve with a majority of 60%, the veto is considered broken. However, what the auditors also check and object to are missing or insufficient amounts in the state budget. In these cases, the Audit Court can also veto the budget.

9.7.3 Citizen concerns

The Audit Court is the central receiving agency for legal matters related to the budget, violations of the Freedom of Information Act, which obliges all ministries to be fully transparent, and questionable awards of state orders. Its auditors investigate independently and follow up on tips from the population. In this respect, the Audit Court is the people's ombudsman when it comes to budgetary issues. It helps voluntary citizens who also check the state accounts via the tax game to see whether complaints are justified. If they are justified, the auditors make sure that the affected politicians listen to them. If this does not take place, or if it takes place inadequately, a justification of the affected politician before his or her electorate can be forced in the budget committee. The head of the Audit Court has the right to summon certain politicians or ministry employees who are responsible for the accounts to appear before the Budget Committee, where they have to give evidence under oath.

10 Central Bank[84]

The Ministry of Finance is responsible for the monetary system. It operates a Central Bank and a Note-issuing Bank for each economic form. The head of the Central Bank and of each Note-issuing Bank are politicians directly elected by the people. The head of the Central Bank of an International Union must be directly elected by the peoples of all member states.

The Central Bank is the bank of the Note-issuing Banks and the State Bank. Its tasks are the implementation of the monetary and financial policy tasks of price stability and full

84§219,1,2 Central Bank and currency policy : BV Art. 99

employment.

10.1 Allocation of money

The Central Bank ensures the constant supply of money to the state and the population. Since there is only one Central Bank for all four economic forms, the Note-issuing Banks are responsible for the different currencies. This applies only to a limited extent to the euro, because this currency is an international currency and Ministries of Finance and Central Banks of other Member States are still involved. The Central Bank has to ensure that there is always an alternative possibility for the population to invest money in the economic forms. This responsibility is assumed by the Central Bank together with the Note-issuing Banks.

10.2 Goals of the Central Bank

The Central Bank sets monetary policy targets. The Note-issuing Banks may set their own targets as long as not all Note-issuing Banks together fail to meet the Central Bank's targets. If the Note-issuing Banks fail to meet the Central Bank's targets, the Central Bank may intervene in their autonomy and set all necessary requirements until the targets are met.

10.2.1 Price stability and full employment[85]

The inflation target is an inflation rate or deflation rate that fluctuates around the 1% mark to ensure price stability. The goal of full employment is considered achieved when the unemployment rate is between 0% and 2%. Both goals are linked to the danger of a wage-price spiral. Higher wages are then not paid through a higher profit share for employees, but passed on to consumers as higher prices. Falling prices can in turn be passed on to employees as falling wages or make the company insolvent.
The rate of wage increase should be higher than the rate of price

---

85§219.6 Central Bank and currency policy

increase. The assumption is that the higher the unemployment, the lower the wages and vice versa. Therefore, the Note-issuing Bank should ensure that when prices rise, the key deposit rates are reduced, and the key issue rates and reserve ratios are increased, or vice versa when prices fall. By tightening the money supply as soon as prices rise, price pressure is imposed on companies because price increases are then punished by the consumer through renunciation and reduced quantity. Through this instrument, the Note-issuing Bank should be able to prevent excessive wages or prices. Wages should only rise in line with the increasing productivity of labour and not due to a rising price level. Prices, in turn, should be in line with wages. Low wages and high prices result in high profits for companies, but lead to a redistribution that creates more poverty than wealth, which is harmful to the national economy. In this case, the Note-issuing Bank can propose the initiative to the responsible Minister of Economic Affairs to adjust the business tax accordingly, so that redistribution via the Unconditional Basic Income can take place in return. The Central Bank can itself call a voting by which the people can determine the business taxes of individual economic forms. This strong intervention in the autonomy of the economic forms, Note-issuing Banks and companies, is reserved for the fight against a wage-price spiral.

The Note-issuing Bank's tools also serve as a threat to get entrepreneurs and employees to demand realistic wages and prices. The Company Auditing Agency, the Antitrust Agency and the responsible Note-issuing Bank monitor whether wages and prices are realistic. The Note-issuing Bank or Central Bank can intervene if necessary.

10.3 Tools of the Central Bank

The Central Bank has tools that Note-issuing Banks do not have because they operate between economic forms or across the economy.

10.3.1 Banknote privilege

The banknote privilege is the exclusive right of Note-issuing Banks to issue banknotes. Banknotes are certificates, coins, digital means of payment or certain in-kind items. By issuing and moving in cash, the amount of cash can be managed. Thus, no Note-issuing Bank can become insolvent because it can create money itself.

The Central Bank can become insolvent vis-à-vis foreign currencies if none of the country's currencies are valuable enough to be able to buy enough currencies of other countries. In this case, the Central Bank restricts its monetary policy to its country's domestic market until purchasing power has increased sufficiently to buy other currencies again.

10.3.2 Debt

The state may only borrow exceptionally and through the People's Bank, by selling government bonds to the nationals. The Central Bank's task is to let the people vote on debt, which usually happens in the budget vote, but can also be asked in a vote called at short notice.

10.3.3 Exchange rates[86]

The Central Bank, in voting with all four Note-issuing Banks, determines the fluctuation band within which the exchange rates of the individual currencies may move. Only if these limits are breached do the Note-issuing Banks have to use their tools of monetary and currency policy, otherwise they are free to do so.

The Note-issuing Banks themselves determine whether the exchange rate moves freely within the fluctuation band, whether it is pegged to another currency or whether it is fixed by the Note-issuing Bank and only adjusted after prior notice. The Barter Economy, with its currency of goods and services, and the Planned Economy, with its currency of labour output per hour, cannot expand their money supply without limits.

---

[86] §219.4 Central Bank and currency policy

The natural productive capacity and the number of humans limit the value of the currency as well as an appreciation and depreciation. An appreciation occurs when more humans become more productive. Devaluation occurs when more humans become less productive. Productivity and number can also separately produce the same effects.

10.3.4 Securities trading / open market transactions

The Central Bank is authorised to buy and sell securities in the form of shares, company bonds and government bonds. Shares and corporate bonds must come from domestic companies, government bonds from member states of the International Union. Securities trading is used when the money supply can no longer be managed by other tools. When buying, newly created money or currency reserves of the affected Note-issuing Bank are used to buy securities on national and, if necessary, international stock exchanges. When the securities are sold, the money supply is reduced again, because the proceeds from the sale are not newly fed into the monetary cycle.

The possibility of being able to reduce the money supply again by selling is the reason why securities are traded by the Central Bank at all. Shares have little effect on the real economy because their price increases the stock market value of the company, but this does not mean that more or less is produced or that higher or lower wages are paid. Corporate and government bonds, on the other hand, result in direct investments that can influence production and wages. The Central Bank has to decide whether it wants to use the tool of open market policy to merely make a value investment to influence the money supply of the banks or whether it wants to fight inflation or deflation on the labour market. In order to influence the labour market, direct state investments in an industry or the population's income are as effective as possible, because the money then arrives directly where the money supply has to be increased in order to fight deflation. The money supply can then be reduced again via other tools, such as the key interest rates or the minimum reserve.

All open market operations are subject to approval. The

people must approve the expenditure, regardless of whether securities are purchased or state investments are made. The people should have a say in which companies or state projects are to be invested in. Thus, in times of crisis, the state can fulfil wishes of the population that would otherwise be rejected as too costly, even though they could raise the standard of living. Co-determination also prevents "moral hazard", i.e. when companies would enrich themselves from state investments.

10.3.5 Currency reserves[87]

Note-issuing Banks have an account with the Central Bank in which they invest foreign reserves in the form of other currencies. The Central Bank has an account in which it holds currency reserves that are invested by the Note-issuing Banks in precious metals or commodities. The money in circulation must be deposited in finite, storable and environmentally sound commodities. The Ministry of Finance watches over this hoard of precious metals and other domestic rare, storable and economically valuable commodities. The stocks of emergency reserves of inputs for an economy, such as grain or petroleum, are created and overseen by the Ministry of Security, but their value flows into the money supply deposit.

The Note-issuing Banks use the income from the interest business to accumulate currency reserves in order to give their banknotes the necessary value. The Central Bank sets the value in voting with the respective Note-issuing Bank. Once the agreed value of the currency has been reached, all further interest income flows into the national budget. The currency reserves are stored at the Central Bank so that it can issue parts of the currency reserves in times of national crisis.

10.3.6 Lender of last resort

The Central Bank assumes the role of lender of last resort in times of crisis. It can thus use the currency reserves of all the country's Note-issuing Banks to support banks, companies

---

87 §219.7 Central Bank and currency policy: BV Art. 99

and private individuals with means of payment in order to maintain confidence in the credit system and banking system. The Note-issuing Banks are the lender of second last resort. They can use their foreign reserves up to a minimum reserve ratio of 50% to manage crises in their respective economic forms.

10.4 Note-issuing Banks[88]

Each economic form is given its own Note-issuing Bank and is its custodian of currency. A Note-issuing Bank is the bank of the banks. Via the Note-issuing Bank, banks can trade with each other and make transfers. For this purpose, each bank receives a bank code as its account number. A bank can invest its assets in its account at the Note-issuing Bank, transfer them to other banks or lend them out to customers. Since there is a Note-issuing Bank for each economic form, each Note-issuing Bank can be more or less independent of the responsible Ministry of Economy. Note-issuing Banks fulfil their purpose of financing the state and reducing taxes with interest rate transactions.

10.4.1 Goals of the Note-issuing Banks[89]

The Note-issuing Banks of the four economic forms guard the different currencies.

In the Barter Economy, care is taken to ensure, on the one hand, that barter traders keep their words of honour and, on the other hand, that there are no scarce goods whose value is traded disproportionately high or, conversely, no worthless surplus goods. The same applies to services in order to be able to guarantee price stability overall. In the Barter Economy, banks are all stocks of consumer goods or production goods. The Note-issuing Bank can only determine human capital in the sense of the educational qualifications of all inhabitants by managing immigration, but not emigration.

---

88 §219,1-4,7,8 Central Bank and currency policy: BV Art. 99
89 §219.3 Central Bank and currency policy

In Planned Economy, the Note-issuing Bank makes sure that the work output per hour is as high as possible and that working hours are not senselessly sat off, but used as productively as possible. The Note-issuing Bank uses the duty roster and the moving out of Experimental Enterprises and Innovation Enterprises for this purpose. The more free time the Social Villagers have and still meet their demand, the stronger the currency. The deposit here is, on the one hand, the human capital of the residents and, on the other hand, the national wealth in the form of the Social Villages including equipment. Reserves in the form of human capital are not possible because no one may be forced to stay or move out for currency purposes. The primary objective of the Note-issuing Bank of Planned Economy is full employment, to which price stability is subordinated.

In the Social Market Economy, the Note-issuing Bank pays attention to a moderate interest rate policy that generates constant interest income, allows a minimal increase in prices, allows wages to rise more than prices and, in order to promote high employment, also tends to accept an increase in prices as long as it is below 2%. The national currency of the Social Market Economy is supposed to generate social redistribution through the devaluation of money by its moderate inflation below 2% and to ensure sufficient money in the credit market, which in the Social Market Economy may only be lent for investment. Economic suggestion or mitigation is done in voting with the Ministry of Social Market Economy.

In the Free Market Economy, the Note-issuing Bank pursues the primary objective of price stability with inflation not exceeding 1%. The Ministry of Free Market Economy is not allowed to influence the Note-issuing Bank. The Note-issuing Bank is part of the European Central Bank and is subject to its requirements. The requirements come from the finance ministers of all member states.

10.4.2 Tools of the Note-issuing Banks

The tools of a Note-issuing Bank can be used differently depending on the type of economic form and the state of the economy. The tools of a Note-issuing Bank are currency reserves, public finance, the deposit and issue base rate, minimum reserve ratio and foreign exchange transactions.

10.4.2.1 Key issue rate[90]

Commercial banks in an economic form can lend money via their account with their Note-issuing Bank and pay the issue base rate, which is set by the Note-issuing Bank. With this money, commercial banks can lend money to companies or private individuals. After a period of time, the money has to be paid back. The interest rates vary depending on the length of the loan. Any amount of money lent out within one day has a higher interest rate than money lent out at a fixed amount for 30 days. Interest payments accrue monthly until the end of the term, or daily in the case of overnight money. The interest payments are earnings that the Note-issuing Banks collect through their interest transactions.

10.4.2.2 Deposit base rate[91]

If a bank's assets are deposited in the Note-issuing Bank's account, a deposit base rate is charged for them, the So-called deposit rate or discount rate. The Note-issuing Bank can pay interest on money deposited if it has lent out more money in total than it has deposited. Accordingly, it generates higher interest income than it has to pay interest. However, if banks are reluctant and do not lend money, they also lend less from the Note-issuing Bank and have to pay fees for depositing money with the Note-issuing Bank. These fees are expressed in a negative deposit rate. Through this instrument, the Note-issuing Bank can influence the banks' lending. With this threat, banks can be persuaded to pursue their business

[90] §219.8 Central Bank and currency policy: BV Art. 99
[91] §219.8 Central Bank and currency policy: BV Art. 99

model on their own initiative and seek out trusting persons and companies that want to venture investments that benefit the humans and bring profits to the banks.

10.4.2.3 Minimum reserve rate

Banks are obliged to hold a minimum reserve ratio set by their Note-issuing Bank. This means that they may never lend out 100% of their money, but must leave a percentage in their account with the Note-issuing Bank. This applies to both equity and debt. Accordingly, it does not matter whether the bank lends out its own money or lends on borrowed money. The minimum reserve ratio must always be deducted from the amount to be lent and paid into the account at the Note-issuing Bank. The same applies vice versa when lent money is repaid.

The minimum reserve rate is created as an allowance on the account, on which interest is paid at 0%. Only above the allowance does the deposit rate apply. The minimum reserves on the banks' accounts mean that in economic crises Note-issuing Banks always have a money reserve that they can spend if necessary.

Through the minimum reserve ratio, the Note-issuing Bank can manage the money supply and avoid excessive bank lending in order to prevent excessive inflation.

10.4.2.4 Foreign exchange transactions

Note-issuing banks can buy foreign or foreigner currencies in order to determine exchange rates. If the currency is to be revalued, other currencies, So-called foreign currencies, are bought. If it is to be devalued, foreign exchange is sold. In voting with the Ministries of Labour and Economic Affairs, the Central Bank can induce the Note-issuing Banks of the economic forms to ensure equalisation through foreign exchange trading between the four Note-issuing Banks. This instrument is only permissible if one or more economic forms have an impact at the expense of one or more other economic forms.

10.5 Living Standard Index

The aim of the Central Bank is to serve the welfare of the people. One of its tasks is therefore to maintain or raise the standard of living for living and future generations. In order to be able to measure the standard of living, statistical data is collected in which human satisfaction or dissatisfaction is expressed. These include economic aspects such as price levels, Gross Domestic Product, unemployment, productivity, income, investment, innovation, wealth distribution, educational attainment, Self-sufficiency, undeclared work, chores, care, DIY, honorary services or hobbies.

Equally included are social aspects, such as partnership, divorce, births, suicides, friendships, life expectancy, health, safety, personal freedom, social security, the rule of law, generational justice, ecology, global prosperity and peacekeeping.

The main task of central and Note-issuing Banks is to determine the Gross Domestic Product and the price level and to manage them with little fluctuation through monetary and currency policy. It is crucial that this policy is used in such a way that other economic and social aspects do not deteriorate. While money and currency policy can only manage two material indicators, they must take into account the effects on the remaining aspects in their decisions.

The Living Standard Index consists of rates and ratios of all individual aspects, on which usually far-reaching statistical data are available. In order to make it easier for the Central Bank and the citizens to observe the effects of changes in one aspect on others and to counteract them if necessary, all necessary data are collected and published at least every 12 months. All aspects are reported in absolute numbers, usually quantities, and how they have changed in percentage terms compared to the previous year. Summarised, this results in the annual Living Standard Index of the country.

10.6 Determination of the Gross Domestic Product

The Central Bank determines the Gross Domestic Product for the entire economy. The Note-issuing Banks determine a Gross Domestic Product for their economic form. The Gross Domestic Product serves as an economic indicator to be able to represent all activities of economic value creation in a monetary value. All unaffordable values, such as unemployment, birth or death, are included in the Living Standard Index. The Note-issuing Banks use their Gross Domestic Product to measure the material prosperity of the citizens who use their economic form.

The Gross Domestic Product is determined in a way that the respective Ministry of Economy determines with the Institute for Evaluation[92] . All necessary data, such as state expenditure and revenues, imports and exports, enterprise data, such as wages, prices, quantities of goods and services sold, investments and wear and tear, are collected by the Company Auditing Agency in its regular audits. The data for the calculation must come from the same period to provide a snapshot of the current economic cycle, usually one month, one quarter and one year. Only the annual calculation of Gross Domestic Product is based on all the data collected to date and on the Company Auditing Agency's audit results for the previous year. The principle is that the economic cycle sets in motion production that produces goods and services that are bought by consumers, giving workers an income to spend or save. By saving it, they open the possibility for persons or companies to invest the money as profitably as possible. Gross Domestic Product is calculated in three ways that must come to the same result:

1. production (also called gross national product)
Gross Domestic Product = Production Value - Intermediate Inputs + Taxes + Tariffs
2. consumption
Gross Domestic Product = Private + State Consumption + Investment + Exports - Imports
3. income (also called national income)

92Ministry of Labour - 20.10 Institute for Evaluation

Gross Domestic Product = Wages of employees + profits of entrepreneurs + depreciation + taxes + tariffs - income from economic activity abroad

The result is an amount given by the Note-issuing Banks in the respective currency. The Central Bank calculates the Gross Domestic Product of the entire economy using the exchange rates at the time of data collection.
With the help of the inflation rate, Note-issuing Banks can determine how sustainable growth really is. If wage-price spirals become obvious, the Note-issuing Bank uses the necessary tools of monetary and currency policy.
The Central Bank compares and rates price developments and Gross Domestic Product of all economic forms and can use its monetary and currency policy tools if necessary.

10.6.1 Barter Economy

The Note-issuing Bank of the Barter Economy determines the Gross Domestic Product from all Barter Economy Zones[93] . The growth of the Barter Economy's Gross Domestic Product is aligned with the growth of nature. Fortunately, natural ecosystems are geared towards growth that humans can help themselves to. Natural resources mostly grow continuously in a linear annual rhythm. The aim of the Note-issuing Bank is not to completely consume the annual growth of animals and plants, which would keep the quantity constant. Nature should be enabled to further expand its capacities. In voting with the inhabitants of the Barter Economy Zone, a growth target is set, up to which nature should grow. This means allowing stocks of animals and plants to grow a little more each year. Even natural growth is not limitless, although human optimisation of natural ecosystems can push the limit upwards. For example, trellises, terraces or irrigation runs can be created to achieve a higher yield per cubic metre of soil per square metre, or more perennial plants can be grown than annuals. When natural growth reaches its limit, humans can increase it through innovation. Economic growth at the

93 Ministry of Barter Economy - 6 Barter Economy Zone

expense of natural growth is prohibited.

In determining the Gross Domestic Product in the Barter Economy, the function of barter traders authenticating their agreements via the People's Computer is used. In the calculation of Gross Domestic Product, this data is accessed to determine quantities and prices of goods and services. The prices are again goods and services in the Barter Economy. Purchasing power parity, the So-called Big Mac index, is used to determine how much labour, time and money a non-internationally tradable good or service costs. The same calculation is made with the identical products in another economic form, region or country. The differences represent the exchange rates.

Only through the exchange rate, which is determined by the Note-issuing Bank, can prices be inserted into the total account of the Barter Economy. The Note-issuing Bank pays particular attention to the prices charged in the wholesale market for goods and services from the Barter Economy. These prices could be higher to collect more foreign exchange or lower because there is an oversupply of the good or service, both within the Barter Economy Zone and in the wholesale market. In case of doubt, sellers are asked for what reason they are selling.

Growth in Gross Domestic Product in the Barter Economy means more natural resources for all inhabitants and increasingly more and more diverse goods and services that can be produced with these resources. In particular, more and more diverse tools, machinery and real estate increasingly increase the efficiency of natural resource use.

10.6.2 Planned Economy

The Note-issuing Bank of the Planned Economy determines the Gross Domestic Product from all Social Villages. The growth of the Planned Economy is linked to the number of inhabitants and productivity. Moving in can be necessarily or voluntarily. The state has no influence on this. Therefore, quantities and prices are subject to constant adjustment. Depending on how many inhabitants there are, they have to do more or less work in order to produce more or less quantities. This data is automatically transmitted to the Note-issuing Bank through the digital duty roster and the goods and services consumed on the Social Villagers' social cards.

Since the currency of Planned Economy is labour output per hour, prices are given in hours. The exchange rate turns them into hourly wages, which can be used to calculate the Gross Domestic Product. The Note-issuing Bank looks at the production time and quality of comparable goods from other economic forms to measure the productivity of the labour force in the Planned Economy. The procedure corresponds to the Big Mac Index of the Barter Economy. Gross Domestic Product can only grow in the Planned Economy if depreciated goods from other economic forms are used or recycled and if productivity can be increased through innovation.

A growth in the Gross Domestic Product of the Planned Economy means more leisure time for the inhabitants with the same or better support for their demand. In particular, more leisure and education lead to increasingly more innovations that can raise productivity and living standards.

10.6.3 Social Market Economy

The Note-issuing Bank of the Social Market Economy determines the Gross Domestic Product from all companies registered in the Social Market Economy, as well as private Self-sufficiency, chores, care, DIY, honorary services, hobbies. These services are included in the Gross Domestic Product at the comparable wage for a similar good or service and published separately. The currency in which Gross Domestic Product is measured is the national currency of the Social Market Economy.

Growth in Gross Domestic Product in the Social Market Economy means growing investment in and consumption of regionally and socially produced goods and services. Health is captured in life expectancy, illness, birth rate and suicide rate and published separately. Growth is achieved by increasing wages but not prices. Prices can remain the same if the same product can be provided more cheaply. This requires innovations that either reduce the number of wage earners, resulting in fewer wage earners receiving higher wages. Or the costs for raw materials or their processing decrease and the same number of wage earners receive higher wages. Higher wages allow more to be consumed or saved. Savings deposits flow into investments for innovations.

10.6.4 Free Market Economy

The Note-issuing Bank of the Free Market Economy determines the Gross Domestic Product from all companies registered in the Free Market Economy. The data for turnover is calculated using the business tax on turnover. The data for wages, prices, quantities and profits, are collected by the Company Auditing Agency as part of its audits. There is an obligation to provide information to the authorities, but not to the public. The distribution of wealth is recorded and published separately. The currency in which the Gross Domestic Product is measured is the Euro.
Growth is achieved by increasing consumption and investment. Limits to growth are only laws that ensure the protection of humans and nature.

10.7 Determination of the price level

Because price developments have a strong influence on exchange rates, the measurement lies with the Note-issuing Bank, which also has the necessary tools to be able to manage price developments as soon as they move outside the Central Bank's prescribed framework. The Ministry of Labour is in charge of collecting the data and how it has to be analysed[94] . The Ministry of Digital Affairs takes care of the data transmission, summarisation and statistical processing in accordance with data protection regulations.[95]
The price level can be calculated in three ways. First, via the

94 Ministry of Labor - 20 Company Auditing Agency, 20.10 Institute for Evaluation
95 Ministry of Digital Affairs - 7 Digital Data Protection, 12 Directories, 6 Statistical Office

quantity equation of money; second, via the Gross Domestic Product deflator; and third, via baskets of goods.

10.7.1 Quantity equation of money

The quantity equation of money is a way to calculate the price level. The change in the price level gives the inflation rate or deflation rate. The price level results from the money supply multiplied by the velocity of money in circulation and divided by real output. Real output is represented by Gross Domestic Product.

With the quantity equation of money, it becomes possible to find out how much money the Note-issuing Banks have to spend in order to achieve equilibrium. By rearranging the individual variables in the equation, the requirements emerge as to how and where the tools of the central and Note-issuing Banks should be used. The quantity equation of money is:

Price level * real output = money supply * velocity of money.

Real output is the Gross Domestic Product minus the inflation rate or the national income or the gross national product. Real output can also be quantified by the number of transactions in the measured period. The value of the transactions is in the money supply.

The money supply results from all the money that has been issued by the Note-issuing Banks so far and how much of it has been lent on by banks and how often. The Note-issuing Banks can specifically influence the money creation multiplier of the banks through the minimum reserve. The Central Bank calculates the total money supply of all Note-issuing Banks and, if necessary, can manage it itself if Note-issuing Banks are unable to do so.

The velocity of money in circulation is mostly constant and only increases in times of strong inflation or slows down in times of strong deflation. The velocity of circulation is measured automatically by analysing digital transactions and scanning the numbers on banknotes as they are deposited by companies and withdrawn by ATMs. An algorithm compares all personal data and calculates the velocity of circulation from the money flows.

10.7.2 Gross Domestic Product deflator

The current Gross Domestic Product is recalculated with prices of a base year. The Gross Domestic Product of the current year is divided by the Gross Domestic Product of a previous year, the So-called base year. To obtain a chained price index, the previous year is always used as the base year. The calculations are carried out for the Gross Domestic Product of all economic forms separately and together. This gives the price index for each and all economic forms.

10.7.3 Shopping baskets

The baskets consist of the full range of goods and services and their prices available through the internet, intranet and Company Auditing Agency audits. The price changes between the current basket and the previous year's basket give the inflation rate. Prices are retrieved monthly and compared with the previous month's prices. The rates of change for the months are added up to the year and divided by 12. These results are also added up and divided by the total number of results. The average rate of price increase is obtained. In order to be able to query different areas of life, there are categories for goods and services.

A basket of goods is created for all essential goods as well as a basket of luxury goods. Deflation is targeted for the basket of essential goods and inflation for the basket of luxury goods. The aim is to keep the overall inflation rate constant at 0%. Luxury goods are always innovative goods that make life better for the user. Better production machines cause the prices of essential goods to fall, while higher prices for development, loans and industrial property rights lead to higher prices.

10.7.4 Innovations

New products appear and old products disappear every year. Therefore, measurements have to be continuously adapted to current purchasing behaviour. The decisive factor here is how changes in quality and innovation are reflected in price, income and production costs. The auditors for technology and innovation identify the price-determining characteristics during their audit and enter them in the audit programme. The technical auditors check the quality of goods and services. During the test, all products are given marks for their quality. If the marks change, the quality of the product has also changed, which is taken into account in the price calculation. With the help of the economic auditors, the technical auditors check what costs are incurred or saved as a result of the change in quality. Deteriorations in quality increase the price, improvements in quality reduce the price. The testing programme stores all inputs and compares them with the actual market prices of these products. The longer data is collected, the higher the probability with which the algorithm can calculate the correlation of changes between quality and price.

The innovation auditors examine the innovations in existing products and new products. The economic auditors' market analysis is used to determine which comparable products are replaced or displaced by the innovation and how the prices of the new and old products change.

In the past, new products had no price to compare with and old products can cost less today. However, because innovation plays a crucial role in the growth of an economy and the standard of living, hedonics[96] is used to calculate price trends. Therefore, a chained inflation rate is used, which indicates the price level in a currency and its change in percent from year to year.

10.8 Measures in the event of inflation or deflation

Inflation or deflation already announce themselves and do not happen overnight, but can be triggered by an event and intensify over time if no countermeasures are taken.

As immediate measures, the key interest rates and the money supply can be raised or lowered. The country's other currencies

---

96https://www.destatis.de/DE/Themen/Wirtschaft/Preise/
Erzeugerpreisindex-gewerbliche-Produkte/Methoden/Downloads/
HandbuchErzeugerpreise.pdf?__blob=publicationFile

provide a further hedge and buy the Central Bank time to react appropriately and in voting with the people. If inflation and deflation are outside the permissible range of fluctuation in the price level, the Central Bank can manage the velocity of money. In the event of inflation, the Central Bank can set a money circulation charge that is levied on every transaction. This reduces the velocity of money in circulation and citizens keep their money longer before spending it again. This lowers the price level and inflation decreases. In deflation, a money circulation premium can be paid to increase the number of transactions. Citizens spend their money again more quickly, thereby increasing the velocity of money in circulation. This raises the price level and deflation decreases. This gives the Central Bank a third tool besides the money supply and the key interest rates.

10.8.1 Inflation

The inflation rate measures the increase in prices, the So-called inflation. Money or other means of payment lose value. Inflation has the advantage that investments become easier because debts lose value in the course of inflation, despite interest. Inflation causes redistribution because the devaluation of money damages those who have a lot of money more. But if humans have very little money, they depend on direct wage payments that adjust daily to prices in order to survive. The tools of central and Note-issuing Banks are more geared towards inflation because inflation suggests consumption or investment. Humans prefer to invest the money in real assets or interest-bearing securities, but their interest rate must be higher than the inflation rate.

Inflation below 5% leads to higher demand for tangible assets or investments that earn higher interest rates than the inflation rate. Above 5% inflation, capital flight occurs because the currency loses value faster than most real assets. The currency is exchanged for other more stable currencies or precious metals. Investments become almost impossible because lending becomes too risky for creditors as long as the interest rate cannot be flexibly adjusted to the inflation rate. Variable interest rates, in turn, are a high risk for companies that choose the interest rate so that it is just below the increase in earnings from the investment. Therefore, from an inflation rate of 5%, the Central Bank has to use its tools to lower inflation. The Note-issuing Banks and, if necessary, the Central Bank manage inflation by increasing the key issue rates, reducing the key deposit rates and tightening the money supply. A price increase can occur through demanders or suppliers.

10.8.1.1 Demand pull inflation

So-called demand pull inflation is triggered by consumers demanding higher quantities than can be produced. This is referred to as home-grown inflation when demand comes from within the country and imported inflation when it comes from abroad. Suppliers respond with higher prices to curb demand. Higher prices can only persist if people spend their money again quickly, increasing the velocity of money in circulation. If the money supply is not increased by the Note-issuing Bank, the price normalises as soon as production capacities are built up.

In times of shortage, the People's Bank can promote the creation of production capacities by granting earmarked loans. The Note-issuing Bank can make a suggestion in its economic form to build up excess capacity in order to be able to react quickly to demand pull-inflation.

10.8.1.2 Supply-pressure inflation

So-called supply-pressure inflation is triggered as soon as production costs rise and are passed on to consumers or when entrepreneurs want to increase their profits. The price increase can only persist if consumers cannot find alternatives for the more expensive product. One speaks of home-grown inflation when higher wages or taxes increase production costs, of imported inflation when the prices of imported raw materials rise.

In supply-pressure inflation, prices also return to normal if the Note-issuing Bank does not increase the money supply and demanders reduce their consumption or switch to other products. If prices do not normalise, the Ministry of Finance can increase taxes on the affected companies and pay out the money collected via the Unconditional Basic Income.

10.8.1.3 Full employment

At full employment, the economy makes full use of its production possibilities. If bottlenecks occur, the price decides which good is produced in exchange for another good. Capacities must be expanded and automated to avoid price increases. Companies that profit from this, because they save on labour costs through automation, give 50% of this to the Ministry of Finance as machine fees. The revenues go 50% to the Unconditional Basic Income and 50% to additional automation until automation accounts for 80% of the Gross Domestic Product output. Automation will eventually produce underemployment unless the population shrinks more than automation grows. To maintain full employment, automation can be managed through the machine charge. The affected Note-issuing Bank can get the Ministry of Finance to make appropriate changes to the machine charge.

10.8.1.4 Imported inflation

When domestic citizens export to foreign countries, they receive foreign currency that is exchanged for the domestic currency. This increases the money supply in the country, but the product with the corresponding equivalent value is abroad. This problem can be solved by more flexible exchange rates.

When imports come from a foreign country with inflation, the prices of imports rise, which can lead to higher wage demands and start the wage-price spiral. This is especially true for goods that are not substitutable, such as oil in the 1970s. To guard against this, the domestic economy should not be dependent on any foreign good. The Company Auditing Agency examines any dependencies and the innovation auditors develop substitute goods together with companies.

10.8.2 Deflation

The opposite of inflation is deflation, which means falling prices and an increase in the value of money or other means of payment. Deflation can occur when the economy is in a downturn. Humans hold on to their money to wait until prices fall further. They hoard money and thus tighten the money supply. As a result, production and wages decrease, which weakens purchasing power.

Deflation always results when a demand gap occurs and excess supply cannot be sold without massive price reductions. Mild deflation increases purchasing power when prices fall and wages stay the same. Deflation becomes dangerous if it lasts for a long time and becomes self-reinforcing, because the Central Bank can then have increasingly less effect with its tools. A deflationary spiral can set in when falling prices lead to falling wages and sales crises lead to layoffs. Incomes fall and consumers buy less in order to save money. But they do not invest it either, because they might need it if they become unemployed soon. Companies invest less because the amount of debt would increase as prices fall, in addition to interest. Because banks know that hardly any company can grow enough through investment to compensate for the deflation rate and the interest rate, they hardly give loans.

10.8.2.1 Exchangeable bonds

In order to increase the money supply gradually and in favour of the affected companies, exchangeable bonds can be issued. The state buys from companies and pays with government bonds, all of which have different maturities. Corresponding interest rates serve as an incentive because this currency yields monthly returns until the full amount is paid at the end of the term. Thus, gradually, the money supply is slowly increased as the government bonds mature. Exchangeable bonds can be applied when consumption, investment, wages and assets decline.

10.8.2.2 Decline in consumption

If people buy fewer products, the supply is higher than the demand and the price falls. Consumption can be influenced by the value added tax. The Central Bank can get the Ministry of Finance to vote on a VAT increase. A VAT increase should be equal to the decrease in prices in order to stop the price decline. This measure serves to signal to market participants that a restraint of consumption or investment due to the expectation of falling prices in the future is unnecessary. In turn, any additional value added tax collected is invested in wages in the industry that is experiencing falling prices.

10.8.2.3 Decrease in investments

If companies do not want to invest their profits in themselves because business is slow anyway, they can decide to invest the money in safe securities. However, this lowers the turnover of the companies that would otherwise have profited from the investment. The investment trap can be solved if securities are taxed more heavily or if companies make investments that have nothing to do with production volume but, for example, with renovation, their own production of raw materials for production, heat or electricity. The innovation auditors provide advice to companies for suitable investments and, if necessary, offer People's Bank loans with a variable term and fixed interest rate.

10.8.2.4 Decrease in assets

If speculative bubbles have caused real estate or securities to experience an excessive price increase, a price decline can follow in a subsequent phase of economic downturn. Those affected feel poorer and spend less. Banks that have granted loans are particularly affected. Debtors fall into over-indebtedness particularly easily in a deflation because it becomes increasingly difficult to repay the same amount with less income. This leads to loan defaults at the banks.

If this liquidity trap opens up because companies demand loans for investment, but commercial banks do not offer loans with the expectation of further falling prices, the Central Bank can intervene. In this case, the People's Bank is entitled to grant loans at 0% interest for investment purposes to domestic citizens and companies that have been previously audited by the Company Auditing Agency.

10.8.2.5 Decline in wages

When prices fall, wages also fall at some point, which sets in motion a downward wage-price spiral that causes the money supply to decrease. The money supply can then be increased by raising the Unconditional Basic Income or by direct state investment in the citizens' desired projects.

10.8.2.6 Decrease in trade restrictions

If tariffs are imposed on products or standards make imports more expensive, lifting them can lead to falling prices. If prices fall in times of deflation, tariffs are raised again.

10.8.2.7 Decline in state expenditure

If state expenditure declines to such an extent that a demand gap is created, prices may fall. The state should announce its spending policy as early as possible so that companies can look for other customers or change their business model. If necessary, state expenditure is increased by issuing new money, which increases the money supply and prices rise.

10.8.2.8 Missing foreign trade

If there is no demand from abroad and the export surplus accounts for a large share of Gross Domestic Product, wages and prices inland can fall. In this case, it is important to increase demand at home in the short term and, in the meantime, to build up a balanced trade account without export surpluses. The economic forms have foreign trade policies with tariffs and export restrictions to protect themselves against foreigner influences. In the short term, their own currency can be devalued to make export goods cheaper.

If the domestic currency appreciates against foreign currencies, domestic products become more expensive for foreigners. They buy less, prices fall. For domestic citizens, imports become cheaper, which leads to a shortfall in demand for domestic producers, and prices fall. To counteract this, tariffs can be lowered for domestic products and tariffs can be raised for foreign products.

When a state is in a currency union, the same effect occurs as with fixed exchange rates. If productivity growth takes place in a member state, the member states must either try to become equally productive or lower their wages in order to be able to lower prices. The member states of a currency union must agree on how to solve the added value of productivity growth in a country. If no solution is found within 6 months, the country with the productivity increase must leave the currency union. The same applies if a country experiences a decline in productivity. In both situations, flexible exchange rates can then lead to a gradual convergence of purchasing power until the affected country can be readmitted to the currency union.

11 People's Bank[97]

The country's state bank is called People's Bank. It is established by the Ministry of Finance to promote the economic and social development of the nation, municipalities and citizens. The head of the People's Bank is directly elected and is responsible for the management of the bank. The People's Bank's business is limited to domestic lending for entrepreneurial purposes and the investment of savings in People's Bank financial products. The People's Bank's primary business partners are nationals, companies and the state. Transactions with foreign countries or foreigners are only permitted in cases prescribed by law and require the approval of the people as soon as they

97§218 State Bank: KV Art.53, §155,5,6 State expenditure

are to be applied.

With its accounts for persons, companies and ministries, as well as exchanges for ideas and the people, People's Bank provides financial services for the domestic money and financial markets. Companies and individuals can have all their accounts with the People's Bank, but they do not have to. They can also use banks of the economic forms as long as they are not in an economic form where only the People's Bank is allowed as a bank.

The People's Bank is the only bank where ministries are allowed to keep their accounts. Citizens and companies manage their taxes through their tax accounts at the People's Bank. In this way, the People's Bank holds the entire state budget and, if necessary, ensures that citizens can lend money to the state in order to partially finance the state budget.

11.1 Accounts

Bank customers have many different accounts at their disposal. Citizens receive their children's account at birth, together with their tax and pension account and the link to the generation account. They can open further sub-accounts. These include the current account, call money account and savings account. As soon as a company is founded, it automatically receives a tax account. Opening further sub-accounts is also possible for companies. The state also has an account with sub-accounts for each ministry, which in turn have sub-accounts for saving or spending money. There is also a work benefit account for Planned Economy and a goods account for Barter Economy.[98] People's Bank accounts are free of charge. Account management can be done in the currencies of the economic forms, money disbursement only in the currencies of the Social Market Economy and Free Market Economy.

There is an unlimited deposit guarantee for all accounts, i.e. in the amount of the total account deposits of all customers. In the event of total account eviction of all customers, the Central Bank's currency reserves must be spent and if that is

98 Ministry of Barter Economy - 12.2 Banks, Ministry of Planned Economy - 8.3 Work benefit account

not enough, loans are taken out on the international financial market.

11.2 Financial services

The People's Bank operates a branch network and a virtual branch that can be visited via the Ministry of Finance intranet site. To offer its customers a wide range of financial services, the People's Bank operates the People's Stock Exchange and the Ideas Stock Exchange. There People's Bank customers can invest in shares, bonds or funds. Companies that are People's Bank customers and the state can issue bonds. The People's Bank operates the People's Fund, Research Cost Fund and Domestic Fund with its own fund managers.

11.3 Foreign trade[99]

All trade with foreign persons, companies or states in which the state is involved is conducted through the People's Bank. This ensures that democratic responsibility can always be claimed by the people from the directly elected head of the People's Bank. Nationals have the opportunity to influence decisions through the veto, repeal and deselection quorum. The People's Bank is the only bank allowed to raise money for the state from abroad by selling domestic or, if necessary, foreign citizens or investors domestic government bonds. The majority of the people must agree to foreign borrowing.

11.4 Change of assets between economic forms

The People's Bank is the only bank authorised to operate in all four economic forms and to hold all currencies available in the country in its accounts. It ensures an equitable transfer of financial assets between economic forms in voting with the ministries of finance, labour and economy. In order to continue to guarantee the people political management, the business of transferring between economic forms may not be

99 §225.7 Foreign trade policy: BV Art. 101

handed over to other banks.

11.5 Citizen account

Every citizen receives an account with the People's Bank together with their birth certificate, including an ATM card. If a citizen lives in Planned Economy, he also has a work benefit account. If a citizen lives in the Barter Economy, he can have his goods included in the goods account. The account for citizens has the following other sub-accounts, all of which cannot go into deficit. If the amount spent exceeds the credit balance, payment is refused.

11.5.1 Current account

The current account is the account for all current revenues and expenditures. From there, credit can be moved to other own accounts, transfers can be made and money can be withdrawn worldwide. Credit balances on this account do not earn interest.

11.5.2 Tax account

All cash withdrawals are taxed via the tax account. Amounts are only ever in this account for a very short time in order to deduct the tax during this booking process. For citizens, value added taxes are levied on all account transactions.

11.5.3 Call money account

Each People's Bank customer specifies an amount to be added to or debited from the current account. The call account is available daily. If the money remains in the call account, this also means being ready to lend the credit balance in the call account for 24 hours the next day. It serves primarily as a government bond with a term of one day. The state guarantees to pay out the full amount at any time within 24 hours, if the client so wishes. Only if all customers want full payment does the state have to go to the international government bond market to take on debts. If the state has no debts, the investment department takes care of the money. The interest rate on the call money account is as high as the inflation rate in the previous quarter. If there is deflation, there is no interest. The interest income is tax-free.

11.5.4 Savings account

The savings account is intended as a deposit account with which citizens can invest their money in People's Bank stock exchanges and funds. With it, they lend their money to domestic companies, research companies and, if necessary, to the domestic state. Shares in funds, shares in companies and bonds can be bought and sold by the state or companies through the savings account. The savings account is considered a company and is subject to the laws of the Social Market Economy. Only profits are taxed, not turnover and therefore no losses. Profit taxes of 20% apply on interest from bonds, dividends from shares, distributions from fund shares and from income from a higher price when selling than when buying.

11.5.5 Children's account[100]

The children's account differs from the citizen's account in that children are not yet legally competent and their parents regulate their finances. All sub-accounts of the citizen account are also possible. The current account is called a children's account until the age of majority. The purpose of the children's account is to prevent parents from having unrestricted access to the child benefit[101] and to give each child as similar a financial starting position as possible. The Ministry of Family Affairs transfers the child benefit to the children's account at the beginning of the month. 1% of the child benefit flows directly into the pension account. The child benefit is primarily used to pay for

---

100 §234.3 Children's rights, child benefit and parental protection
101 Ministry of Family Affairs - 8.4 Child benefit

care services for the child. Only if there is a balance left over from the child benefit at the end of the month may parents use the child's bank card to purchase goods and services for the child. Vendors may only charge age-appropriate products for the child on the child benefit card.

11.5.6 Pension account

5000 euros are transferred to the pension account by the Ministry of Finance for the birth. The starting capital of 5000 euros comes from the liquidation of a pension account of a deceased citizen. When the account is closed, the initial capital is paid back first. The aim is not only to increase the initial capital by the rate of inflation in the long term, but also to let the population become richer and richer over generations. The annual interest rate corresponds to the annual growth rate of the domestic Gross Domestic Product minus the inflation rate. In voting with the Central Bank and the Note-issuing Banks, the People's Bank may also decide that the balance in the pension account shall bear interest at the base rate of the Free Market Economy's Note-issuing Bank if the account is kept in euros, or at the deposit base rate of the Social Market Economy's Note-issuing Bank if the account is kept in the national currency of the Social Market Economy. No money can ever be withdrawn from this account until pension, only any amount of money can be deposited at any time. Thus, the compound interest effect ensures a higher final amount. How much each citizen gets paid out at the end of his working life depends on how well the people have worked together, which is reflected in the growth rate of the Gross Domestic Product or the prime interest rates. The compound interest effect increases exponentially. As an example, assume a human life of 80 years, the amount increases as follows: If the Gross Domestic Product grows by 1% per year, the starting capital doubles after 80 years, at 2% it quadruples, at 3% it increases tenfold and at 5% the starting capital is 50 times as high. This is an incentive for individuals to contribute as a whole and to keep the value of money stable so that the Central Bank's increase in the money supply does not cause the Gross

Domestic Product to grow.

Two types of payout are possible at retirement. Firstly, you can have the interest payments paid out monthly from that day. This removes the compound interest effect, but interest continues to be paid on the total amount, which is not touched. The remaining amount is transferred to the generation account upon death. The second method of payment is a loan granted by People's Bank to the pensioner. The amount of the credit corresponds to the balance in the pension account at retirement. The interest on the credit is equal to the interest on the balance of the pension account. However, since the compound interest effect continues to act on the full amount of money even after retirement, the credit balance on the pension account increases slightly more than the loan amount. As soon as the pensioner dies, the loan is settled by the credit balance on the pension account and the remainder is transferred to the generation account. No matter which method of payment is chosen, it is made via the tax account, where the value added tax is deducted.

If all the money is spent too soon, before you die, you have to move to the Social Village and work where you can until you die. Of course, this is only an emergency if you have never provided for your pension in any other way or if you have no family that wants to help.

Any surplus, whether due to earlier death or frugal living, is transferred tax-free to the family's generation account. This happens as soon as the pension account together with the citizens' account is closed upon receipt of the death certificate.

11.5.7 Generation account

The generation account is in one family name and can be transferred to another family name upon marriage. Each family member has an admission to the generation account, each child receives an admission at birth. Only payments can be made into the generation account. Only the interest earned can be paid out as a pension or wage subsidy if all family members agree. If the family members cannot agree, the interest income flows equally to all who have an admission.

The income flows into either the current account or the pension account. This is decided by the person who receives the payment. Value added tax is due when the payment is made from the current or pension account. Interest income is taxed at a profit tax rate of 20%. The interest rate is equal to the growth rate of the Gross Domestic Product after deducting the rate of inflation or deflation.

11.6 Company account

Every company that is established in the People's Bank or opens a branch inland is given a People's Bank company account. The tax account is automatically set up as a sub-account. Owners of the company are granted an admission and can grant admission to other employees of the company. If companies manage their accounts only through People's Bank, they can take out loans. A credit line of 10% of the balance of all sub-accounts, except the current account, is granted. Credit may only be granted to companies to enable sales growth or to research, purchase and introduce innovations.

11.6.1 Current account for companies

The current account can be used to make all incoming and outgoing transfers as well as business payments in and out. Business payments are wages for employees, salaries for owners and payments to suppliers of goods and services that the company needs to offer its products. Amounts from the savings account must first be posted to the current account in order to be used.

11.6.2 Tax account for companies

The tax account is linked to all accounts the company has with other banks. From the company account at People's Bank, only the current account is linked. Through the links, all deposits and withdrawals are diverted via the tax account. The amounts are only in the tax account for milliseconds until the tax has been deducted and therefore do not earn interest. For cash transactions, companies must use cash registers[102] , which automatically send data on their revenues and expenses to the tax account. When the cash is deposited, the taxes calculated by the cash registers are deducted.

The links automatically show when it is a deposit, a transfer between company accounts or a payment. Depending on whether the company pays sales tax or profit tax, different deductions are made.

For sales tax, all payments into company accounts are taxed immediately.

For profit tax, all incoming and outgoing payments for the month are recorded, the outgoing payments are deducted from the incoming payments and profit tax is levied on the result, provided the amount is positive. Accordingly, losses are not taxed. The tax account debits the company account with the corresponding amount at the end of the month.

Ministries of economy using a profit tax can decide whether or not to tax wages for employees and salaries for owners. If wages are to be taxed, the tax deduction must be made before the monthly payment of wages. If salaries are to be taxed, owners may only pay themselves their profits after the tax deduction.

11.6.3 Savings account for companies

The savings account is intended for the company to earn returns from its savings after deducting business tax. Savings accounts of the entrepreneurs are for investing money to be invested in the company in the future. Withdrawal for profit taking is not allowed, for this purpose there is the Citizen's Savings Account.

Companies can invest savings amounts in the Ideas Stock Exchange, the Research Cost Fund or the People's Fund. Direct investment in People's Stock Exchange shares or bonds is not possible to avoid market power.

Returns from interest on bonds and dividends on shares flow into the savings account via the tax account, where 20%

102Ministry of Digital Affairs - 13.6.9.2 Cash register

profit tax is deducted. Returns are further invested to benefit from the compound interest effect. As soon as entrepreneurs want to invest these savings in the company, they can transfer the desired amount from the savings account to the current account.

11.7 State account

The state account consists of current accounts and savings accounts for each ministry. Self-administered ministries must also maintain their accounts with the People's Bank, unless they also have the Ministry of Finance under municipal self-administration, in which case it is voluntary. All receipts and payments are processed through the current accounts. Revenues from profits of state enterprises and fees flow into the savings account. The investment department takes care of investing the money in the savings account and transfers returns back to the savings account. In the course of the budget vote, 25% of the amounts in the savings account are distributed to the ministries, 25% to their employees and 50% to the state budget. Amounts allocated by the budget vote are posted to the ministry's current account and can be posted from there to the savings account until used. The ministries determine the deadline by which certain amounts may be invested by the investment department. There is no tax account for the government account, because no taxes are due.

11.8 People's Stock Exchange

The People's Stock Exchange is designed to allow nationals to invest in domestic companies or their state and to prevent fluctuations by foreign investors. A lower volume of capital is accepted in order to exclusively strengthen the purchasing power in the country. In order to effectively strengthen purchasing power, only nationals living in the country may invest in companies whose owners are nationals who also live in the country and offer their products. Only companies from the Planned Economy and Social Market Economy, state enterprises and People's Innovation Company are allowed to offer their shares and bonds on the People's Stock Exchange. Investing money can strengthen purchasing power with low risk because Social Market Economy companies have outage insurance, downturn insurance and insolvency insurance.[103] Planned Economy companies are Innovation Enterprises or Experimental Enterprises that transform into a Planned Economy joint-stock company to be able to enter the market economy with the seed capital from the stock exchange.[104] The companies are constantly audited and advised by the Company Auditing Agency in order to be as profitable as possible in the long term. This reduces the risk for investors.

Shares and bonds are traded on the People's Stock Exchange. Resale to other stock exchanges or foreigners is prohibited. The companies that trade their shares and bonds on the People's Stock Exchange do not have any requirements regarding size, turnover or profits. The Exchange Commission[105] inspects the companies before and after the initial public offering to ensure that all requirements are met. The Company Auditing Agency is obliged to publish all audit results of companies that issue and have issued shares and bonds. The same applies to ministries that issue and have issued government bonds.

11.8.1 Trade

The trade works via the People's Bank savings account. There is an interactive search mask in the form of the map of the inland, where you can have the companies displayed sorted by colour according to industry. In addition to the sector, the search functions also include the turnover, profits, number of employees and the value of the company. All this data is presented in tabular and graphical form per year and goes back to the initial public offering of the company. This data is provided by the Company Auditing Agency. Investors can use the search to select companies that currently issue bonds or

103 Ministry of Social Market Economy - 17.5.6 Outage insurance, 17.5.7 Downturn insurance, 10.2 Insolvency insurance
104 Ministry of Planned Economy - 10.6 Innovation Enterprise, 10.8 Experimental Enterprise, 13.4 Planned Economy Joint-stock Company
105 Ministry of Labour - 18.3.3 Exchange Commission

shares. If shares or bonds are owned by People's Bank savings customers and the customers want to sell their shares or bonds to other People's Bank savings customers, these shares and bonds will also appear in the search. If a company issues shares or bonds and investors want to sell their shares, multiple prices are displayed unless investors or companies set the same price. Sellers of shares and bonds must specify a price at which they are willing to sell. They can choose whether they can sell immediately at this price or whether the highest bidder buys in an English or Dutch auction. In an English auction, the auction starts at this price and if no one outbids the highest bid for 2 minutes, the item is sold. In a Dutch auction, the price drops every minute from the starting bid. Each seller can set the price himself and is shown the current median of all prices submitted so far for a share or bond of the company as a guide.

11.8.2 People's shares

Company shares traded on the People's Stock Exchange are called people's shares. They do not have a fixed term. The shareholder can hold them as long as he wants. The shares have a profit share called a dividend, which is paid out once a year. The shareholder receives a registered share. His name is automatically retrieved from the People's Bank savings account when he buys and is deposited with the company. At the annual shareholders' meeting, shareholders have the right to information, the right to approve or dismiss the board of directors and the right to elect the managing directors.

11.8.3 People's bonds

Loans traded on the People's Stock Exchange are called People's Bonds. They have a fixed term and a fixed interest rate, which is paid out annually, quarterly or monthly. At the end of the term, the full amount is repaid. Bonds can be issued by the state or by companies. There is no minimum amount, any amount is possible. The person issuing bonds determines the start date and end date, how much the interest is, in what instalment it is paid and what amount is needed. Companies and ministries are only allowed to borrow in order to increase or decrease their capacity to meet demand or to become more innovative and increase productivity. All this information is necessary to create a bond in People's Bank's bond forum. The bond is automatically linked to the company's profile in the Labour Directory, where all the audit results of the past 3 Company Auditing Agency audits are also stored. Once the amount of money the company or the state needs is reached, this bond is closed. The page then states when the next bond is expected to be issued. Every saver involved is credited with the interest on his deposited amount as soon as a month, quarter or year has expired. Bonds are tradable on the People's Stock Exchange and can be resold to other domestic People's Bank savings account holders.

Savings account holders can diversify a self-selected portion of their savings in bonds. A minimum amount is not specified. In the interactive search mask, they can search for companies as they are used to from the Labour Directory, namely by industry, products or services. However, only companies and ministries that have just launched a bond and still have bonds available until the desired loan amount is met, or bonds whose launch date is still in the future, are displayed. Investors should preferably know the sectors in which they are investing. It is therefore possible to have one's own knowledge and interests automatically analysed from the other directories and use them as search filters. You select an industry, service or product and are shown in your People's Bank account home screen as soon as a company from your election area issues a bond.

11.8.3.1 Government bonds

Government bonds must first be floated on the People's Stock Exchange. Only if they do not find sufficient buyers there may the Ministry of Finance, after approval by the people, sell government bonds on the international financial market and forward the amount to the affected ministry. On the People's Stock Exchange, ministries may issue bonds themselves if the people have given their consent. Government debts are supposed to be debts that the state owes to its people. Together with the people, it generates added value from the capital, from which all citizens in the country benefit and with which the interest is paid. The People's Bank, as the people's bank, is there to turn state debts into debts that the state has with the people and thus only has to pay its own people the interest on the debt, which in turn strengthens purchasing power.

For government bonds, the interest rate paid is the growth rate of the Gross Domestic Product of the previous year. To introduce this system, no interest is paid at all in the first year. In the following years, the interest rate then remains the same for one year.

Example: Germany Gross Domestic Product growth per year and in % of growth compared to previous year

Year	2005	2006	2007	2008	2009	2010
%	0,7	3,7	3,3	1,1	-5,6	4,1

2011	2012	2013	2014	2015
3,7	0,4	0,3	1,6	1,7

As you can see, there can also be a negative development. In this case, no interest is paid at all, but only one year later. Thus, government bonds also act as a counter-cyclical economic stimulator. The term of the government bonds is determined by the respective ministry.

11.8.3.1.1 Real estate bonds

The Ministry of Infrastructure issues its own government bonds as needed to build properties through the Construction Team[106] . When the property is sold to the owners, 10% of the profits accrue to the Ministry of Infrastructure and the rest is paid out to the creditors as interest on a quarterly basis. Apart from the Construction Team, only companies of the Social Market Economy may participate in the construction, provided they are paid with money from the real estate bond. If a Social Market Economy company involved becomes insolvent or unable to perform, the insolvency or outage

---

106Ministry of Infrastructure - 5.8 Construction Team

insurance[107] kicks in and another Social Market Economy company can complete the house. In this way, the bonds are protected and the construction projects are implemented so that there can be a refund of the initial amount.

11.9 Ideas Stock Exchange

The Ideas Stock Exchange administers and trades all financial resources that are used to remunerate inventors and investors or to support companies that import innovations. Only naturalised persons, nationals and domestic companies may invest on the Ideas Stock Exchange. The trade, investment products and companies are regularly audited by the Exchange Commission and innovation auditors.[108] A profit tax of 20% is levied on the earnings, which is deducted when the money is transferred from the savings account to the current account.

11.9.1 Innovation bonds

First, innovation bonds are used to provide money to start-up companies to finance market entry costs. Secondly, they can be used by existing companies that import an innovation to finance the launch costs. In both cases, investors are entitled to a return, which is agreed as a percentage interest rate before the deposit, and repayment of all the money invested. The repayment date can be postponed in voting with the investors. Through People's Bank's interactive investment platform on the intranet, debtors can contact their creditors directly. If the company becomes insolvent, the invested money is lost.

11.9.2 Innovation shares

Companies can issue innovation shares for their innovations. They are checked by the innovation auditors to see if they are feasible and have gone through a cost calculation. The

107 Ministry of Social Market Economy - 17.5.6 Outage insurance, 10.2 Insolvency insurance
108 Ministry of Labour - 18.3.3 Exchange Commission, 20.7.5 Innovation auditor

company or companies specify how much money they need to be able to use the innovation in the company. Accordingly, they set the price and the number of shares they will issue. In the first week of marketing, no shares are traded yet, but they are pre-ordered through the Ideas Directory[109] . Since the company or companies have indicated their cost of access to the market, the price of the share falls during that week as more People's Bank savings account holders order this innovation share and rises when people cancel their orders during the week. The price they have to pay is set at the end of the week, as is the number of shares that will be issued. This means that if few people buy the shares, each share has to cost more to reach the desired amount. If more people buy shares, more humans share the cost. In this respect, the shares are auctioned because buyers and sellers can see at any time when they order the share how many people have done so so far and what the current purchase price would be.

The innovation shares entitle the holders to be involved annually in the profits that accrue to the company through the innovation. This profit sharing is distributed as a dividend. It is limited to 50% of the additional profits. Further rules for the distribution of profits may differ in the various economic forms. Shareholders are not entitled to voting rights in the management of the company. If the company becomes insolvent, the money invested is lost.

11.9.3 Licence share

One can buy licence shares. For example, a 0.1% share in a licence for 180 euros, which creates a right to 0.1% of the licence fee. The inventor can thus bring all or part of his industrial property right to the Ideas Stock Exchange. The money raised can then be used to set up a company that produces the invention under licence and pays a licence fee. Licensors can also bring parts of their royalty entitlement to the exchange. These royalties are split up and paid out to the owners of a royalty share as a dividend.

If the innovation fails, you lose your money. These shares are

109 Ministry of Innovation - 8 Ideas Directory

not shares in the company, but shares in the industrial property right, which is also a property that can generate profits. In this respect, the dividend of this share is also only a share in the added value that this invention generates for the company or companies. The user of the invention must therefore pay out a licence fee annually as a dividend to all shareholders. The amount of this dividend, or the licence fee, depends on the turnover generated by the invention. During the annual audit by the innovation auditors of the Company Auditing Agency[110] , the profits are determined and the dividend is set.

11.9.4 Period of validity

The innovation bonds, innovation shares and licence participation shares can be traded on the Ideas Stock Exchange as long as the industrial property right is maintained or expires at the end of the maximum protection period. The annual fee for maintaining the industrial property right is included in the licence fee when licensing via innovation shares or licence participation shares and is deducted from the total amount when paid out to the shareholders.

11.9.5 Product shares

Product shares are shares in an innovative product that is so expensive that consumers prefer to rent it rather than buy it. Inventors can create a profile for the product in the Ideas Directory. There, potential shareholders can express their interest. The price of a share is equal to the production costs for the product divided by the number of buyers of the share. The product is produced to order. If there are enough shareholders to produce the product, it is produced and rented out. Shareholders thus form a community of buyers who jointly vote to determine where the product is to be produced and repaired, how high the rental price is and to whom the product is rented. The buyer community

---

110 Ministry of Labour - 20.7.5.4.2 Measuring the profit share through innovation

gets in touch with each other via the product's profile in the Ideas Directory and forms a group. The inventor brings the product to the Ideas Stock Exchange as soon as it is on the market. Founding shareholders who were already in the Ideas Directory keep their shares, but can also sell them on the Ideas Stock Exchange from then on. Trade on the international market is permitted. As soon as enough shareholders can be found, another product can be produced and thus further product shares can be issued. Interested shareholders report via the product's profile in the Ideas Directory and as soon as a sufficient number of buyers is reached, the product is ordered. The sufficient number depends on how much each buyer is willing to pay. The more buyers there are, the cheaper a share can become. Shareholders with a low willingness to pay buy only one share, shareholders with a high willingness to pay buy several shares. The rental price is calculated from the costs of operating and maintaining the product plus the dividend for the shareholders.

11.10 Risk

The risk class indicates the probability of losing part of the money invested or, in the worst case, suffering a total loss. The higher the risk class, the higher the risk of default. Conversely, the returns in higher risk classes are also higher.
The risk of losing money invested on the People's Stock Exchange is low compared to traditional international stock exchanges. Bonds issued by Social Market Economy companies and the state have the lowest risk class, followed by shares in Social Market Economy companies. All these asset classes are covered by insurance against default, economic fluctuations and insolvency.[111] The next highest risk class is bonds and shares of Experimental Enterprises, followed by Innovation Enterprises. The Ideas Stock Exchange ranks in the highest People's Bank risk class with its investment products. If the companies listed on the Ideas Stock Exchange do not belong to the Social Market Economy, there is no insurance unless

111 Ministry of Social Market Economy - 17.5.6 Outage insurance, 17.5.7 Downturn insurance, 10.2 Insolvency insurance

the company has also purchased such insurance. The lowest risk is in innovation bonds. Only if the innovation fails do creditors suffer a loss. With innovation shares, the dividend may be low and other investors may rate the innovation low, which lowers the selling price of a share. Product shares and licence participation shares depend on the sale of the licence or the rental of the product.

In order to spread the risk, investors also have the option of investing small amounts. In addition, People's Bank offers funds that are administered by fund managers from the investment department in order to buy rising and safe shares and bonds as far as possible and sell falling or uncertain ones.

11.11 Funds

The investment department forms funds from the investment products of the People's Bank and Ideas Stock Exchange, in which holders of a People's Bank savings account can invest. The more money that flows into a fund, the more shares or bonds are bought and vice versa. The advantage of funds lies in investment amounts of any size and the possibility of not having to constantly follow the economic development of an industry or a company. A 20% profit tax is due on income from fund units, which is deducted when the money is transferred from the savings account to the current account.

11.11.1 People's Fund

The People's Fund is a mixed fund consisting of individual sub-funds. When investing in the People's Fund, investors can either specify fixed allocations in which sub-funds their money is invested, or they can invest their savings amount in the People's Fund as a lump sum. The apportionment is done by the fund managers of the investment department. The sub-funds are equity, bond and index funds.

11.11.1.1 Equity funds

The equity fund consists of an Exchange-Traded Funds and an administered fund. Fund investors do not have voting rights at the shareholders' meeting, nor do the fund managers.

For the Exchange-Traded Funds, all shares that are represented in the index are automatically purchased. The amount of shares is determined by the size of the company compared to the other companies in the index. For example, few shares are bought from a small company with low sales and profits and vice versa. The index consists of all companies that have issued people's shares. For the automated fund management, all necessary data is retrieved from the Company Auditing Agency audits.

The administered fund consists of companies that are selected by the fund manager of the investment department. In the selection process, fund managers take care to choose companies that are profitable on the one hand and on the other hand have a role in the national economy that raises the standard of living in the long term. When money is invested in administered funds, a profit tax of 1% is paid to the investment department via the profit tax, which then amounts to 21%. The fund managers obtain their information from the auditors of the Company Auditing Agency.

11.11.1.2 Bond funds

Bond funds are also called bond funds in the finance economy. The bond fund also consists of an Exchange-Traded Funds and an administered fund. The Index-Traded Funds works with the following adjustments, like the Index-Traded Funds for shares. All companies and ministries that have issued bonds are represented in the index. The amount of bonds in the Exchange-Traded Funds is equal to the total volume of a bond. For example, only a few bonds are bought from companies that want to raise a small amount with bonds and vice versa.

The administered fund works like the administered equity fund. In the case of the bond fund, however, it is not the companies that are considered, but the projects that are to be financed with the amount. Here, the fund managers make sure that the amount invested has as high an impact as possible, causing an increase in turnover or profits and productivity. Preference is given to projects that have a positive impact on an entire industry, the national economy or the environment.

11.11.2 Real estate funds

People's Bank's real estate fund is closed, but can additionally issue bonds if there is a lack of money. Only People's Bank customers with a savings account can take out a building savings contract to invest in the fund. The desire to own a property must be connected with the investment. Although the interest income flows to the building society, it cannot be withdrawn. The savings are repaid in the form of a property. Should the treaty be terminated, the amount can be transferred from the savings account to the current account, incurring 20% profit tax.

11.11.2.1 Building savings contract

The building savings contract is a sub-account of the savings account into which only deposits can be made. Here, citizens and companies can save money for construction projects tax-free. All these savings are permanently available to the Ministry of Infrastructure for its housebuilding programme.[112] Through the money of all building savers, properties are continuously built and sold by hire-purchase or directly. The sales price is a maximum of 15% above the construction costs, in the hire-purchase procedure a maximum of 20%. A maximum of 10 percent of the profits go to the Ministry of Infrastructure and 5 to 10 percent flow annually to the building savers as interest. The term ends with the completion of the own property, whereby the amount is not paid out but is used in the own property.
The housebuilding programme is also used later to build one's

---

112 Ministry of Infrastructure - 5.13 Housebuilding programme

own property. Citizens and companies describe as precisely as possible where and how the property is to be built. They can enter postcode areas, square metres, construction type and furnishings, if possible also in different construction forms. For example, residents can state that they would like to live in both a flat and a house, with or without a garden or balcony. The input mask is taken from the Real Estate Directory.[113] The more precise the information provided by the citizens or companies, the better the Ministry of Infrastructure can plan the construction projects. The Construction Team does not only build individual buildings, but directly entire settlements with residential and commercial buildings. If the redevelopment or reconstruction of a neighbourhood is desired in a city, the planning of the construction project takes place in voting with the inhabitants of the city. As soon as a sufficient number of citizens or companies in an area want to have a property and have saved up enough money in the building savings contract, the Ministry of Infrastructure contacts them to plan the building project. Since the housebuilding programme also offers real estate on a hire-purchase basis, it is not necessary to have the entire amount in the building savings contracts that is needed for construction. The remaining amount is financed through real estate bonds. In this case, however, the rent increases by the interest for the bond in the hire-purchase procedure.

If the amount of money in the building savings contract is not sufficient to pay for a property by the time of death, the amount is bequeathed to the direct descendants in equal shares. If there are no descendants, the money goes into the housebuilding programme.

11.11.3 Domestic funds

The People's Bank operates the domestic funds for foreigners with its fund managers in the investment department. There is one fund per industry that buys shares and bonds of the companies in that industry. The volume may not exceed 10 per cent of the total volume. This means that only 10 per

113 Ministry of Infrastructure - 4.5.1 Real Estate Finder

cent of the issued shares of a company may be sold to the domestic fund. For bonds, it means that only 10% of the total amount of bonds may be financed by the sale of bonds to the domestic fund. This 10% shortage prevents a price bubble for nationals, who would be forced out of the market by foreign millionaires' excessive willingness to pay. Likewise, foreigner influence on company management is to be prevented in this way. The domestic fund is not allowed to bid on the issue of shares or bonds by companies. It may only buy shares or bonds sold to it by People's Bank savings customers. When buying, the domestic fund always pays at least the average price of all sales prices of that share or bond over the past 12 months.

11.12 Investment Department

In this department, the best investment bankers in the country are gathered and given admission to the data of the Company Auditing Agency and domestic state universities. They are allowed to make requests to auditors and professors to improve the research work. They automatically execute savings account investments, create algorithms for successful investment strategies in cooperation with the Company Auditing Agency, and administer People's Bank funds.

11.12.1 State investment

In order to distribute the investments of the state savings fairly, the Ministry of Finance issues the following regulations. The rating agency[114] examines the investments and gives risk assessments, which can also prevent a purchase. The total capital is divided and in order to spread the risk, investments are made in 5 different areas. 20% is invested in the international financial market, but not in weapons or food. 20% is invested in shares of the 20 largest domestic joint-stock companies in the Free Market Economy. 20% will be invested in shares of the 20 largest domestic Social Market Economy joint-stock companies. 20% is invested in start-ups of the Ministry of

114 Ministry of Labour - 18.4 Rating Agency

Innovation. 20% will be invested in real estate of the Ministry of Infrastructure. In the long term, the interest income from the assets will contribute to tax reduction.

11.12.2 Staff of the Investment Department

In order to find new talented employees, each student of finance and economics is given start-up capital to invest as profitably as possible. A college student is given the task of turning 1000 euros into more during his studies. If he breaks off his studies, he has to pay it all back. If he finishes, he only has to pay back 1000 euros and 10% of the profits he made from it. If he has lost money, he only has to pay back the remaining amount. The students who have made the most money from the 1000 euros get a job offer in the investment department of the People's Bank.

Like all citizens, college students also have an account with the People's Bank. There, another sub-account is opened for them, into which the starting capital is paid. From this account, all investments in the financial market can be made, which are also available to the People's Bank investment department. The user interface and options of the investment programme are as identical as possible. This gives college students the same opportunities as People's Bank investment bankers, only they work with less start-up capital. Access rights to Company Auditing Agency data are restricted and anonymised.

12 Switching to the new system

The Ministry of Finance is responsible for the changeover of the procedures for determining the national budget as well as for setting up the four Note-issuing Banks and the People's Bank. In cooperation with the Ministry of Digital Affairs, it links the statistics to the new economic indicators.

12.1 Tax Offices

The Tax Offices will be dissolved and all files digitised. The only Tax Office will be located in the capital city of the Ministry of Finance. The real estate of the Tax Offices is converted or auctioned off in voting with the population. Most of the workers transfer to the Company Auditing Agency and are given a company car and a home office for their work. The staff who have uncovered the most tax fraud in their careers move to the tax auditors. Qualified auditors move to the economic auditors of their election. Excess staff capacity is reduced through timely layoffs or retirement without backfilling.

12.2 Tax restructuring

Compensation for regions is abolished. Taxes on income, companies and assets will be abolished and replaced by the business tax. The entrepreneurs will be asked in which economic form they would like to run their company in the future, once all four ministries of economy have been established.

Sales tax and real estate transfer tax will be abolished and replaced by value added tax without double taxation. The current value added tax is levied as usual, but uniformly at 20%, no matter what, and it is no longer deductible. It also applies to foreigners and is levied as tariffs.

Property tax, inheritance tax and gift tax remain in place until the first generation is debt-free. This means that the state budget is saved for the coming year and no more state debt is outstanding.

All revenues that previously went to the nation, regions or municipalities go to the national Ministry of Finance to be distributed by the people in the budget vote. Municipalities become municipalities and regions can form a union of municipalities to administer their budget independently.

All citizens and companies will have a tax account with the People's Bank. After the tax restructuring, no more tax returns have to be filed. Losses and expenses cannot be deducted. The aim is to record all revenues and expenses made in the country once and tax them immediately, without the need for staff to process tax returns. Until cash registers are introduced, companies are obliged to deposit their cash once a week at any People's Bank branch and receive change of the desired value free of charge.

12.3 Legislative reforms

Laws on real estate joint-stock companies with listed shares are abolished and replaced by a ban on real estate joint-stock companies with listed shares. All affected joint-stock companies will have to offer their real estate on a hire-purchase basis and will be compensated for this.

The Reorganisation Tax Act is reformulated because companies now have only one form, which differs in the four economic forms.[115] The law serves as a draft for ministries of economy when they regularise the switching of companies between economic forms by law.

12.4 Introduction of the People's Bank

The People's Bank is formed from the state banks and state shares in private banks. The shares in private banks are sold to citizens to make it a cooperative bank of the Social Market Economy. If there are not enough buyers, the shares and branches become the responsibility of the People's Bank. The staff and branches are retained, provided there is no other branch of a state-owned bank within a radius of 5 kilometres. The management boards, supervisory boards and corporate headquarters, including departments such as investment banking, will be merged and only the best bankers will remain. The best investment bankers from the former state-owned banks are pulled together into the investment department of the Directory. The supervisory board is now the people, because all the numbers can be published and questioned on the intranet on the Ministry of Finance's site. The managing director is directly elected by the people.

115https://de.wikipedia.org/wiki/Umwandlungssteuergesetz

12.4.1 Statutory pension insurance

The state pension scheme will be transferred to the Social Market Economy pension scheme and all previous savings will be transferred to the pension account, so that the people's previous savings will be with the People's Bank and not with an insurance company of the Social Market Economy. Tax subsidies for pensions will be abolished. Pensioners in poverty can live in the Social Villages.

12.5 Nationalisation and privatisation

All state holdings in economic foundations and companies are sold unless they are brought in to fulfil a task in the new system. Transport routes will be re-nationalised and taken over by the Ministry of Infrastructure. Telecommunications companies will be re-nationalised and taken over by the Ministry of Digital Affairs. The printing press for passports and identity cards will be re-nationalised and continued as a Planned Enterprise. The most capable state consultants from private companies are recruited and move to the Company Auditing Agency business consultants. The administration for the sale of state assets will continue as a Planned Enterprise, which will recycle decommissioned state assets for further use in the Planned Economy. Digital portals to domestic laws are replaced by the Law Directory of the Ministry of Justice.

12.6 Debt conversion of existing public debt abroad

Many countries are currently in debt. A large part of this national debt is held abroad, the rest by domestic banks and insurance companies. The interest on the debt is a burden on the national budget every year. First of all, all persons living inland are asked to transfer their account management and that of their company to the cost free accounts of the People's Bank. The savings of the domestic population should be able to cover the foreign debt.

The deposits of all citizens and companies in People's Bank accounts create deposits that are used as private government bonds. All deposits of all citizens' accounts and business accounts with the People's Bank, except the savings account, earn interest at the average rate of 2.5%, which so far has gone to creditors. The People's Bank's minimum reserve ratio is 5% and unlimited deposit insurance applies. Capital is only raised on the international financial market if the deposit insurance is paid out. Once all foreign debt has been transferred to the domestic market, the interest payment then no longer flows abroad, thus strengthening purchasing power at home, which increases Gross Domestic Product and removes dependence on foreign investors. Debt conversion continues until all foreign government debt is only held directly by domestic residents or companies and, in particular, the interest on the debt is distributed directly to the citizens or companies. If this goal cannot be fully achieved because too few nationals transfer too little financial assets to their accounts at the People's Bank, insurance companies will be served first, followed by domestic citizens.

New government bonds, i.e. government debt, are issued through People's Bank savings accounts. Thus, the citizens set the short-term debt ceiling through their deposits with the People's Bank. The state is only allowed to incur debts if the people agree. The aim is to get rid of all debts as quickly and safely as possible. In the short term, the aim is to transfer the debts from abroad to the domestic market. In the medium term, all debts should be paid off. In the long term, savings should be created. As soon as savings have been created that cover the national budget for an entire year, a nationwide folk festival is celebrated for one day.

12.7 Conversion of the old ministries

All departments and units that transfer to the Ministry of Finance are listed below. If only the department or sub-department is named, all its units are transferred. If individual units are named, only those units are transferred. All departments and units not named are dropped. Existing staff adapt their tasks to the new requirements. The corresponding names of the units can usually be found as keywords in the running text.

12.7.1 Federal Ministry of Finance[116]

I A Fundamental issues of finance and economic policy
Fundamental and structural issues of tax policy, research and policy advice, public finances, tax estimation, analyses of the economy, growth and tax revenues

I B Fundamental issues of individual economic sectors/ sustainability
Fundamental issues of the business economy including SMEs and innovation, the labour market, housing and regional politicians, sustainability and quality of public finances, fiscal policy issues of economic development (domestic guarantees), demographic development.

II Federal budget

III Customs, sales tax, excise duties
Customs law, import turnover tax, market regulation law, energy tax, electricity tax, nuclear fuel tax, greenhouse gas quota, excise duties on luxury foodstuffs, motor vehicle and air transport tax
Sales tax and transaction taxes - national and international, insurance tax, sales tax, taxability, entrepreneur, place of supply, tax base, tax rates, invoice, input tax deduction, record-keeping obligations, sales tax control and fraud prevention - national and international

IV Tax Department - Direct Taxes
Tax policy, tax reform, fundamental issues of tax law, coordination of tax legislation projects, environmental tax and duty policy, tax procedural law, tax advice, tax simplification, tax enforcement, organisation and automation, financial transaction tax (FTT), tax procedural law and Fiscal Code, Fiscal Court Code, equity regulations, notification obligations of the authorities, Tax Code

---

116https://www.bundesfinanzministerium.de/Content/DE/Downloads/ Ministerium/organigramm.pdf?__blob=publicationFile&v=27 Status: 01.05.2019

(accounting regulations, external audits, criminal tax law), effects of tax policy on public budgets and tax burden distribution, automation in federal tax administration, coordination of requirements for federal automation procedures Interface for Information Technology-related legislation with the "Information Technology Supply" department, data protection
Taxes on income and earnings, corporate tax policy, transfer taxes, inheritance tax, property tax, rating income from capital assets, renting and leasing, capital gains tax, investment tax law, REIT law, corporate taxation, corporate income tax, trade tax, reorganisation tax law, determination of profits, income from trade and self-employment, balance sheet tax law, reorganisation tax law special expenses

V Federal financial relations, state and constitutional law
Financial relations with the federal states and municipalities, state and constitutional law, financial constitution, federal-state financial relations Financial affairs of the municipalities, federal fiscal equalisation, proceedings before the Federal Constitutional Court and ECtHR, international law
Legal matters, Freedom of Information Act, public procurement law and procedures, equalisation of burdens

VII C Financial market stability, guarantees, debt management

VIII A Real estate and privatisation

VIII B Participation management
Fund holdings, RAG Foundation, Deutsche Post AG, Deutsche Telekom AG, Bundesdruckerei and Toll Collect, PD -Berater der öffentlichen Hand GmbH and VEBEG, Autobahn GmbH and juris

VIII C Infrastructure and contaminated site management
Deutsche Bahn AG and subsidiaries, euro cash coins

12.7.2 Federal Ministry of Justice and Consumer Protection[117]

III Trade and Commercial Law
Partnership law, corporate law, tax law

IV Constitutional and Administrative Law, International and European Law
Financial constitutional law

117https://www.bmjv.de/SharedDocs/Downloads/DE/Ministerium/
Organisationsplan/Organisationsplan_DE.pdf;jsessionid=A807B5B1F5E
FC74825E8B2A6508405BE.2_cid297?__blob=publicationFile&v=131
Viewed on: 14/05/2019

Contact form

Dear reader
If you would like to make what you have read come true, in whole or in part, together with other like-minded people, I offer you several possibilities with this contact form. Fill it out, tear out the page and send it by post to:
Andreas Seidl, P.O. Box 1206, 63488 Seligenstadt / Germany

Or send the details to:
Phone: 0049 1522 818 2243 (whatsapp, telegram, signal)
Email: andreas.seidl2022@web.de

Please mark with a cross:
O   I want to found a dynamic People's Party.
O   I want to donate money for implementation.
O   I want contacts with like-minded people in my area.

Forename: _____

Surname: _____

Please fill in only the contact option through which a reply should be made.

Street, house no.: _____

Postcode, city, country: _____

Phone: _____

Email address: _____